SMALL BUSINESS CONSIDERATIONS, ECONOMICS AND RESEARCH

SMALL BUSINESS LENDING

CREDIT AVAILABILITY AND MARKET CONDITIONS

SMALL BUSINESS CONSIDERATIONS, ECONOMICS AND RESEARCH

Additional books in this series can be found on Nova's website under the Series tab.

Additional e-books in this series can be found on Nova's website under the e-book tab.

BUSINESS ISSUES, COMPETITION AND ENTREPRENEURSHIP

Additional books in this series can be found on Nova's website under the Series tab.

Additional e-books in this series can be found on Nova's website under the e-book tab.

SMALL BUSINESS CONSIDERATIONS, ECONOMICS AND RESEARCH

SMALL BUSINESS LENDING

CREDIT AVAILABILITY AND MARKET CONDITIONS

BARBARA SCHWARTZ
EDITOR

NOVINKA

New York

For permission to use material from this book please contact us:
Telephone 631-231-7269; Fax 631-231-8175
Web Site: http://www.novapublishers.com

Library of Congress Cataloging-in-Publication Data

ISBN: 978-1-62417-480-3

Published by Nova Science Publishers, Inc. † New York

CONTENTS

PREFACE

This book details the extent of small business lending by all creditors and identifies factors that give policymakers insight into the small business credit market, including the demand for credit by small businesses; the availability of credit; the range of credit options available; the types of credit products used; the credit needs of small businesses; and the risks of lending to small businesses.

Chapter 1 - Section 2227 of the Economic Growth and Regulatory Paperwork Reduction Act of 1996 requires that, every five years, the Board of Governors of the Federal Reserve System submit a report to the Congress detailing the extent of small business lending by all creditors. The act specifies that the study should identify factors that give policymakers insight into the small business credit market, including the demand for credit by small businesses, the availability of credit, the range of credit options available, the types of credit products used, the credit needs of small businesses, the risks of lending to small businesses, and any other factors that the Board deems appropriate.

Between 2007 and 2012, the years covered by this chapter, financial markets experienced extraordinary stresses. Conditions in financial markets began deteriorating in 2007 and worsened dramatically in the fall of 2008. As the financial crisis intensified, the U.S. economy entered a recession. The financial crisis and the recession negatively affected credit flows to businesses for several reasons, including tight lending conditions that restricted the supply of credit by financial institutions, reduced investment opportunities that depressed the demand for funds by businesses, and the deterioration of the financial health of potential borrowers. Since the recession ended in the second quarter of 2009, overall lending conditions and credit flows have improved for businesses, but improvement has been slower for small businesses.

The concerns of the Congress and other policymaking bodies about small business financing largely stem from the perception that small firms have more difficulty gaining access to credit sources than do large businesses or other types of borrowers. The source of this difficulty may be that lending to small businesses is generally considered riskier and more costly than lending to larger firms. Compared with larger firms, small businesses are much more sensitive to swings in the economy and have a much higher failure rate. In addition, lenders historically have had difficulty determining the creditworthiness of applicants for some small business loans. The heterogeneity across small firms, together with widely varying uses of borrowed funds, has impeded the development of general standards for assessing applications for small business loans and has made evaluating such loans relatively expensive. Lending to small businesses is further complicated by the "informational opacity" of many such firms. Little, if any, public information exists about the performance of most small businesses because they rarely have publicly traded equity or debt securities. Many small businesses also lack detailed balance sheets and other financial information often used by lenders in making underwriting decisions.

Up-to-date and comprehensive information about the universe of small businesses is sparse, and most evidence about financing needs and sources is derived from surveys. In response to the financial crisis and ensuing economic turmoil, the National Federation of Independent Business (NFIB) sponsored surveys in 2009, 2010, and 2011 to gauge the credit access of small firms during this period. The surveys show that, among small businesses, larger firms were more likely than smaller firms to use traditional sources of credit such as lines of credit and business term loans, and declines in usage between 2009 and 2011 were strongest for the smallest firms. However, whether this pattern reflects a greater need for credit at larger firms or whether lenders are simply more willing to extend credit to larger firms is unclear. The relationship between firm age and credit use is similar to the relationship between size and use, with declines in usage between 2009 and 2011 being most apparent for the youngest firms.

In addition to traditional sources of credit, many small businesses rely on alternative means of financing, including credit cards and trade credit. These widely used alternative forms of credit may be important both in financing small businesses and, as substitute products, in influencing the demand for traditional credit by small firms. According to the NFIB surveys, just under 60 percent of small firms used a credit line or business loan in each year, but nearly 90 percent used a credit card or trade credit. Although the vast majority of small firms used credit cards or trade credit, a large percentage of these firms paid their outstanding balances on time, suggesting that much of the use of these products was for convenience rather than for longer-term financing of expenses.

In some cases, small businesses may have wanted to use more credit than was reflected in the survey, but were unable to obtain it. According to the NFIB surveys, one-half of small businesses applied for some type of credit in 2009, and just over one-half of these applicants were successful in obtaining all or most of the credit for which they applied. The application rate in 2010 was similar to that in 2009, but the approval rate increased, with nearly two-thirds of firms obtaining all or most of the credit for which they applied. In 2011, the fraction of firms applying for credit increased more than 8 percentage points over 2010, but success rates declined to a level similar to that observed in 2009.

Besides the firms that were denied credit, some firms that may have wanted additional credit may not have applied for it because they anticipated that their applications would be denied. The NFIB surveys asked respondents whether they had forgone applying for needed credit because of the expectation of denial. The data indicate that there may have been a large number of "discouraged borrowers" over this period; in 2009, more than one-third of the sample reported having forgone applying for credit for this reason. While this fraction declined a bit over time, it remained at about 30 percent in 2011, a level that seems elevated relative to earlier periods.

Overall, credit use by small business has declined in recent years. This decline is likely due to a combination of several supply and demand factors. First, the demand for credit started to decrease in late 2006, plummeted in 2008, and has only recovered partially since then. Second, credit generally became less available as banks tightened their standards. Finally, small businesses' financial health and their ability to pay their bills in a timely fashion have generally deteriorated over this time, making it more difficult to borrow, even if the firms desired to do so.

Small businesses obtain credit from a wide range of sources, including commercial banks, savings institutions, finance companies, nonfinancial firms, and individuals such as a family member or a friend. According to the 2003 Survey of Small Business Finances, depository institutions, which include commercial banks, savings institutions, and credit unions, supplied credit to more than three-fourths of the businesses that reported having outstanding credit. Nondepositories, which include both financial and nonfinancial firms, provided credit to about one-third of small businesses in 2003. More-current data suggest the continued importance of commercial banks as providers of credit to small businesses in recent years.

Because banks are the leading source of credit to small business, much attention has been paid to developments in banking that may influence credit availability. The substantial consolidation of the banking industry over the past 25 years is one such development. Mergers and acquisitions have dramatically reduced the number of banks, thereby increasing the importance of large institutions and the concentration of industry assets. These changes to the structure of the industry have raised concerns about possible reductions in the availability of credit to small businesses because large banks tend to be proportionately less committed than smaller banks to small business lending.

The evidence suggests that small banks continue to account for a meaningful share of small business lending activity measured by holdings of business loans equal to or less than $1 million (small) and equal to or less than $100,000 (microloans). In 2011, banks with assets of $250 million or less accounted for 66.8 percent of all banking organizations but only 4.0 percent of all banking assets. However, they held 13.7 percent of all small business loans and 13.9 percent of business microloans. In addition, the results of studies that directly analyze the relationship between consolidation activity and the availability of credit to small businesses tend to suggest that although mergers and acquisitions may sever existing bank firm relationships and may introduce some short-term uncertainty, overall they have not reduced credit availability to small businesses. After a merger, any reduction in small business lending by the newly consolidated bank is generally offset by an increase in small business lending by other banks.

The relevant market for many small business loans remains local. The structure of the local banking market is particularly important because changes in concentration could affect the level of competition for small business lending, which, in turn, could influence the cost of borrowing and the quantity of credit demanded. The data show that despite the significant amount of consolidation in the banking industry, local banking markets do not appear to have become less competitive. Generally, in rural, micropolitan, and metropolitan statistical area markets, the number of banks and offices has remained constant or increased somewhat, whereas the Herfindahl-Hirschman Indexes have either remained constant or decreased somewhat. Modest deconcentration, in conjunction with a small increase in the number of banks, suggests that a reduction in competition from commercial banking organizations is not likely to have been a contributing factor in the decline in the availability of credit in recent years.

Savings institutions, defined as savings banks and savings and loan associations, provide much less credit to small businesses than do commercial banks. As of June 30, 2011, the value of small business loans held by savings institutions was slightly more than one-tenth of the value held by banks. The differences between the lending volumes of the two groups reflect both differences in the number of institutions (1,057 savings institutions versus 5,670 commercial banking organizations) and differences in their business models.

Credit unions, which are not-for-profit financial cooperatives that are owned and controlled by the people who use their services, offer many of the same financial services that banks do. Like savings institutions, credit unions have not historically provided a great deal of credit to small businesses. However, credit unions have become a more important source of small business loans in recent years. Although outstanding small loans to businesses by credit unions remain a small fraction of those by commercial banks, they have increased steadily throughout the recession and post-recession period, while commercial banks' small loans to businesses have declined. Between 2007 and 2011, credit union outstanding loans to business members *increased* by 54.5 percent, while outstanding small loans to businesses by commercial banks *decreased* by 11.1 percent.

In recent years, nondepository institutions have become increasingly important sources of financial services to small businesses. The 2009 NFIB survey reported less than 2 percent of businesses using something other than a bank, credit union, or savings and loan as their primary financial institution. This share more than doubled by 2011, when 5.0 percent of firms reported having a nondepository primary financial institution. In addition, firms may receive credit from institutions that are not their primary financial institution, likely making the shares of firms reporting them as a primary financial institution a lower bound for their total usage.

Support for small business development has been a priority of policymakers for several decades, and federal, state, and local agencies have sponsored programs that assist in channeling capital to small business. Several long-standing government initiatives exist to help support credit access for small businesses, particularly small businesses owned by historically underserved groups such as women and minorities. Two such initiatives of particular importance are the Community Reinvestment Act (CRA) and various loan programs sponsored by the Small Business Administration

(SBA). The CRA was enacted in 1977 to encourage federally insured depository institutions to help meet the credit needs of their local communities, particularly low- and moderate-income neighborhoods, consistent with safe and sound operations. The SBA provides financing to young and growing small firms through several channels such as the 7(a) Loan Program and SBA 504 Certified Development Companies. Among the policy objectives of the SBA loan programs are the goals of promoting entrepreneurship opportunities for women and minorities.

Additional support for small businesses has come in the form of new legislation. The American Recovery and Reinvestment Act of 2009 and the Small Business Jobs Act of 2010 both provided resources to small businesses through increasing credit availability, providing capital to small business lenders, and putting in place tax cuts for small businesses. The most recent piece of small business legislation is the Jump-start Our Business Startups Act. Signed into law in early April of 2012, this bill is intended to make it easier for start-ups and small businesses to raise funds, especially through crowd funding online. This legislation is a departure from the two earlier bills, as it is focused on access to finance through less conventional channels.

Securitization is the process of packaging individual loans and other debt instruments, converting the package into a security, and enhancing the credit status or rating to further the security's sale to third-party investors. The securitization of small business loans has the potential to substantially influence the availability of credit to small businesses, but the obstacles to securitizing small business loans are large. Securitization generally has thrived in markets in which the costs of acquiring and communicating information to investors about loans and borrowers are low. Most small business loans cannot readily be grouped into large pools that credit agencies and investors can easily analyze: Loan terms and conditions are not homogeneous, underwriting standards vary across originators, and information on historical loss rates is typically limited. The information problems associated with small business loans can be overcome, or offset to a degree, by some form of credit enhancement, as in the case of the SBA's 7(a) loans. However, the more loss protection needed to sell the securities, the smaller are both the net proceeds from the sale of the securities and the incentive for lenders to securitize their loans. Small business loans are an asset for which the high transaction costs of providing credit enhancements have made many potential securitizations unprofitable.

Despite these obstacles, between 2002 and 2007, securitization of small business loans increased at a moderate pace each fiscal year. Then, in late

2008, the securitization markets nearly collapsed. As the secondary markets froze and regulators attempted to restore financial stability, several actions were undertaken, with important implications for small business loan secondary markets. While the secondary markets for SBA 7(a) loans and 504 debentures have largely returned to pre-crisis functionality, securities not backed by an SBA guarantee continue to struggle.

There is always a high degree of churning in the small business population, with firms going in and out of business. However, during the recent period, the rate of new business formation has declined. What has caused the lack of activity is not clear. There has been much speculation that the decrease in home prices—and consequently home equity has constrained potential entrepreneurs' ability to finance new businesses. However, existing business owners consistently report that lack of demand and economic uncertainty are the largest problems facing their business in recent periods, not access to capital. The lack of demand, increased uncertainty, or both could have caused fewer business ideas to have a positive expected value and thus fewer businesses to be formed. Nonetheless, it does seem likely that the home price declines had some effect on the number of firms established over the recent period.

Overall, between 2007 and 2012, credit conditions for small businesses underwent substantial change. Favorable supply conditions prevailed until 2008, when such conditions tightened and demand fell. As the recession ended, supply conditions improved but demand remained weak. By 2012, credit flows to larger businesses had essentially returned to their pre-recession levels, while credit flows to small businesses, though improved, remained well below those levels.

Chapter 2 - Credit markets normally recover slowly following financial crises, and the most recent episode was no exception. However, after declining throughout 2009 and much of 2010, recent measures of aggregate credit outstanding have shown some signs of improvement. Nonrevolving consumer credit outstanding, which includes auto and student lending, has increased for the past seven months. Issuance of corporate bonds has been robust for several quarters, and new issuance of commercial mortgage-backed securities picked up in the first quarter of 2011, albeit from very low levels. Commercial and industrial (C&I) loans outstanding have resumed growing modestly on average.

While credit availability seemed to improve for large companies throughout the past year, small businesses still complained of difficulty in gaining access to credit. Recent anecdotes lead me to believe that conditions are improving for small businesses, but data are scarce for this market. Today I will pull together information from a variety of sources, including surveys of small businesses and surveys of lenders, to paint a picture of the credit conditions currently facing small businesses.

In: Small Business Lending
Editor: Barbara Schwartz

ISBN: 978-1-62417-480-3

Chapter 1

REPORT TO THE CONGRESS ON THE AVAILABILITY OF CREDIT TO SMALL BUSINESSES*

Board of Governors of the Federal Reserve System

EXECUTIVE SUMMARY

Section 2227 of the Economic Growth and Regulatory Paperwork Reduction Act of 1996 requires that, every five years, the Board of Governors of the Federal Reserve System submit a report to the Congress detailing the extent of small business lending by all creditors. The act specifies that the study should identify factors that give policymakers insight into the small business credit market, including the demand for credit by small businesses, the availability of credit, the range of credit options available, the types of credit products used, the credit needs of small businesses, the risks of lending to small businesses, and any other factors that the Board deems appropriate.[1]

Between 2007 and 2012, the years covered by this chapter, financial markets experienced extraordinary stresses. Conditions in financial markets began deteriorating in 2007 and worsened dramatically in the fall of 2008. As the financial crisis intensified, the U.S. economy entered a recession. The financial crisis and the recession negatively affected credit flows to businesses

* This is an edited, reformatted and augmented version of a report to Congress by the Board of Governors of the Federal Reserve System, dated September 2012.

for several reasons, including tight lending conditions that restricted the supply of credit by financial institutions, reduced investment opportunities that depressed the demand for funds by businesses, and the deterioration of the financial health of potential borrowers. Since the recession ended in the second quarter of 2009, overall lending conditions and credit flows have improved for businesses, but improvement has been slower for small businesses.

The concerns of the Congress and other policymaking bodies about small business financing largely stem from the perception that small firms have more difficulty gaining access to credit sources than do large businesses or other types of borrowers. The source of this difficulty may be that lending to small businesses is generally considered riskier and more costly than lending to larger firms. Compared with larger firms, small businesses are much more sensitive to swings in the economy and have a much higher failure rate. In addition, lenders historically have had difficulty determining the creditworthiness of applicants for some small business loans. The heterogeneity across small firms, together with widely varying uses of borrowed funds, has impeded the development of general standards for assessing applications for small business loans and has made evaluating such loans relatively expensive. Lending to small businesses is further complicated by the "informational opacity" of many such firms. Little, if any, public information exists about the performance of most small businesses because they rarely have publicly traded equity or debt securities. Many small businesses also lack detailed balance sheets and other financial information often used by lenders in making underwriting decisions.

Up-to-date and comprehensive information about the universe of small businesses is sparse, and most evidence about financing needs and sources is derived from surveys. In response to the financial crisis and ensuing economic turmoil, the National Federation of Independent Business (NFIB) sponsored surveys in 2009, 2010, and 2011 to gauge the credit access of small firms during this period.[2] The surveys show that, among small businesses, larger firms were more likely than smaller firms to use traditional sources of credit such as lines of credit and business term loans, and declines in usage between 2009 and 2011 were strongest for the smallest firms. However, whether this pattern reflects a greater need for credit at larger firms or whether lenders are simply more willing to extend credit to larger firms is unclear. The relationship between firm age and credit use is similar to the relationship between size and use, with declines in usage between 2009 and 2011 being most apparent for the youngest firms.

In addition to traditional sources of credit, many small businesses rely on alternative means of financing, including credit cards and trade credit. These widely used alternative forms of credit may be important both in financing small businesses and, as substitute products, in influencing the demand for traditional credit by small firms. According to the NFIB surveys, just under 60 percent of small firms used a credit line or business loan in each year, but nearly 90 percent used a credit card or trade credit. Although the vast majority of small firms used credit cards or trade credit, a large percentage of these firms paid their outstanding balances on time, suggesting that much of the use of these products was for convenience rather than for longer-term financing of expenses.

In some cases, small businesses may have wanted to use more credit than was reflected in the survey, but were unable to obtain it. According to the NFIB surveys, one-half of small businesses applied for some type of credit in 2009, and just over one-half of these applicants were successful in obtaining all or most of the credit for which they applied.[3] The application rate in 2010 was similar to that in 2009, but the approval rate increased, with nearly two-thirds of firms obtaining all or most of the credit for which they applied. In 2011, the fraction of firms applying for credit increased more than 8 percentage points over 2010, but success rates declined to a level similar to that observed in 2009.

Besides the firms that were denied credit, some firms that may have wanted additional credit may not have applied for it because they anticipated that their applications would be denied. The NFIB surveys asked respondents whether they had forgone applying for needed credit because of the expectation of denial. The data indicate that there may have been a large number of "discouraged borrowers" over this period; in 2009, more than one-third of the sample reported having forgone applying for credit for this reason. While this fraction declined a bit over time, it remained at about 30 percent in 2011, a level that seems elevated relative to earlier periods.

Overall, credit use by small business has declined in recent years. This decline is likely due to a combination of several supply and demand factors. First, the demand for credit started to decrease in late 2006, plummeted in 2008, and has only recovered partially since then. Second, credit generally became less available as banks tightened their standards. Finally, small businesses' financial health and their ability to pay their bills in a timely fashion have generally deteriorated over this time, making it more difficult to borrow, even if the firms desired to do so.

Small businesses obtain credit from a wide range of sources, including commercial banks, savings institutions, finance companies, nonfinancial firms, and individuals such as a family member or a friend. According to the 2003 Survey of Small Business Finances, depository institutions, which include commercial banks, savings institutions, and credit unions, supplied credit to more than three-fourths of the businesses that reported having outstanding credit.[4] Nondepositories, which include both financial and nonfinancial firms, provided credit to about one-third of small businesses in 2003. More-current data suggest the continued importance of commercial banks as providers of credit to small businesses in recent years.

Because banks are the leading source of credit to small business, much attention has been paid to developments in banking that may influence credit availability. The substantial consolidation of the banking industry over the past 25 years is one such development. Mergers and acquisitions have dramatically reduced the number of banks, thereby increasing the importance of large institutions and the concentration of industry assets. These changes to the structure of the industry have raised concerns about possible reductions in the availability of credit to small businesses because large banks tend to be proportionately less committed than smaller banks to small business lending.

The evidence suggests that small banks continue to account for a meaningful share of small business lending activity measured by holdings of business loans equal to or less than $1 million (small) and equal to or less than $100,000 (microloans).[5] In 2011, banks with assets of $250 million or less accounted for 66.8 percent of all banking organizations but only 4.0 percent of all banking assets. However, they held 13.7 percent of all small business loans and 13.9 percent of business microloans. In addition, the results of studies that directly analyze the relationship between consolidation activity and the availability of credit to small businesses tend to suggest that although mergers and acquisitions may sever existing bank firm relationships and may introduce some short-term uncertainty, overall they have not reduced credit availability to small businesses. After a merger, any reduction in small business lending by the newly consolidated bank is generally offset by an increase in small business lending by other banks.

The relevant market for many small business loans remains local. The structure of the local banking market is particularly important because changes in concentration could affect the level of competition for small business lending, which, in turn, could influence the cost of borrowing and the quantity of credit demanded. The data show that despite the significant amount of consolidation in the banking industry, local banking markets do not appear to have become less competitive. Generally, in rural, micropolitan, and metropolitan statistical area markets, the number of banks and offices has remained constant or increased somewhat, whereas the Herfindahl-Hirschman Indexes have either remained constant or decreased somewhat. Modest deconcentration, in conjunction with a small increase in the number of banks, suggests that a reduction in competition from commercial banking organizations is not likely to have been a contributing factor in the decline in the availability of credit in recent years.

Savings institutions, defined as savings banks and savings and loan associations, provide much less credit to small businesses than do commercial banks. As of June 30, 2011, the value of small business loans held by savings institutions was slightly more than one-tenth of the value held by banks. The differences between the lending volumes of the two groups reflect both differences in the number of institutions (1,057 savings institutions versus 5,670 commercial banking organizations) and differences in their business models.

Credit unions, which are not-for-profit financial cooperatives that are owned and controlled by the people who use their services, offer many of the same financial services that banks do. Like savings institutions, credit unions have not historically provided a great deal of credit to small businesses. However, credit unions have become a more important source of small business loans in recent years. Although outstanding small loans to businesses by credit unions remain a small fraction of those by commercial banks, they have increased steadily throughout the recession and post-recession period, while commercial banks' small loans to businesses have declined. Between 2007 and 2011, credit union outstanding loans to business members *increased* by 54.5 percent, while outstanding small loans to businesses by commercial banks *decreased* by 11.1 percent.[6]

In recent years, nondepository institutions have become increasingly important sources of financial services to small businesses. The 2009 NFIB survey reported less than 2 percent of businesses using something other than a bank, credit union, or savings and loan as their primary financial institution. This share more than doubled by 2011, when 5.0 percent of firms reported having a nondepository primary financial institution. In addition, firms may receive credit from institutions that are not their primary financial institution, likely making the shares of firms reporting them as a primary financial institution a lower bound for their total usage.

Support for small business development has been a priority of policymakers for several decades, and federal, state, and local agencies have sponsored programs that assist in channeling capital to small business. Several long-standing government initiatives exist to help support credit access for small businesses, particularly small businesses owned by historically underserved groups such as women and minorities. Two such initiatives of particular importance are the Community Reinvestment Act (CRA) and various loan programs sponsored by the Small Business Administration (SBA). The CRA was enacted in 1977 to encourage federally insured depository institutions to help meet the credit needs of their local communities, particularly low- and moderate-income neighborhoods, consistent with safe and sound operations. The SBA provides financing to young and growing small firms through several channels such as the 7(a) Loan Program and SBA 504 Certified Development Companies. Among the policy objectives of the SBA loan programs are the goals of promoting entrepreneurship opportunities for women and minorities.

Additional support for small businesses has come in the form of new legislation. The American Recovery and Reinvestment Act of 2009 and the Small Business Jobs Act of 2010 both provided resources to small businesses through increasing credit availability, providing capital to small business lenders, and putting in place tax cuts for small businesses. The most recent piece of small business legislation is the Jump-start Our Business Startups Act. Signed into law in early April of 2012, this bill is intended to make it easier for start-ups and small businesses to raise funds, especially through crowdfunding online. This legislation is a departure from the two earlier bills, as it is focused on access to finance through less conventional channels.

Securitization is the process of packaging individual loans and other debt instruments, converting the package into a security, and enhancing the credit status or rating to further the security's sale to third-party investors. The securitization of small business loans has the potential to substantially influence the availability of credit to small businesses, but the obstacles to securitizing small business loans are large. Securitization generally has thrived in markets in which the costs of acquiring and communicating information to investors about loans and borrowers are low. Most small business loans cannot readily be grouped into large pools that credit agencies and investors can easily analyze: Loan terms and conditions are not homogeneous, underwriting standards vary across originators, and information on historical loss rates is typically limited. The information problems associated with small business loans can be overcome, or offset to a degree, by some form of credit enhancement, as in the case of the SBA's 7(a) loans. However, the more loss protection needed to sell the securities, the smaller are both the net proceeds from the sale of the securities and the incentive for lenders to securitize their loans. Small business loans are an asset for which the high transaction costs of providing credit enhancements have made many potential securitizations unprofitable.

Despite these obstacles, between 2002 and 2007, securitization of small business loans increased at a moderate pace each fiscal year. Then, in late 2008, the securitization markets nearly collapsed. As the secondary markets froze and regulators attempted to restore financial stability, several actions were undertaken, with important implications for small business loan secondary markets. While the secondary markets for SBA 7(a) loans and 504 debentures have largely returned to pre-crisis functionality, securities not backed by an SBA guarantee continue to struggle.

There is always a high degree of churning in the small business population, with firms going in and out of business. However, during the recent period, the rate of new business formation has declined. What has caused the lack of activity is not clear. There has been much speculation that the decrease in home prices—and consequently home equity has constrained potential entrepreneurs' ability to finance new businesses. However, existing business owners consistently report that lack of demand and economic uncertainty are the largest problems facing their business in recent periods, not access to capital.[7] The lack of demand, increased uncertainty, or both could have caused fewer business ideas to have a positive expected value and thus fewer businesses to be formed. Nonetheless, it does seem likely that the home price declines had some effect on the number of firms established over the recent period.

Overall, between 2007 and 2012, credit conditions for small businesses underwent substantial change. Favorable supply conditions prevailed until 2008, when such conditions tightened and demand fell. As the recession ended, supply conditions improved but demand remained weak. By 2012, credit flows to larger businesses had essentially returned to their pre-recession levels, while credit flows to small businesses, though improved, remained well below those levels.

Flows and Terms of Business Credit

Between 2007 and 2012, the years covered by this chapter, financial markets experienced extraordinary stresses. Conditions in financial markets began deteriorating in 2007 and worsened dramatically in the fall of 2008.[8] As the financial crisis intensified, the U.S. economy entered a recession. The financial crisis and the recession negatively affected credit flows to businesses for several reasons, including tight lending conditions that restricted the supply of credit by financial institutions, reduced investment opportunities that depressed the demand for funds by businesses, and the deterioration of the financial health of potential borrowers. Since the recession ended in the second quarter of 2009, overall lending conditions and credit flows have improved for firms, but the improvement has been slower for small businesses.

Aggregate Business Financing

Nonfinancial business debt growth, which recorded double-digit percentage growth rates in 2006 and 2007, slowed sharply over 2008 and became negative in 2009 (figure 1, panel A).[9] Debt growth rebounded slowly in 2010 and has picked up more significantly since then. As a result, the ratio of nonfinancial business debt to gross domestic product reached record levels in 2008 but has since drifted down (figure 1, panel B).

Gross equity issuance by nonfinancial firms has also fallen notably since 2007 (figure 1, panel C). Public equity issuance, through both initial and seasoned offerings, which had maintained a moderate pace by historical standards from 2002 to 2007, dropped in 2008 but rebounded to its pre-crisis levels in 2009. In contrast, private equity issuance, which had increased sharply in the years preceding the financial crisis, dropped in 2009 and 2010 and has since maintained a moderate pace. In 2006 and 2007, the rate of equity retirements through cash-financed mergers and share buybacks was booming, resulting in substantially negative net equity issuance. However, equity retirements plummeted in 2008 and especially 2009 before rebounding in 2010 and 2011. As a result, net equity issuance, which remained negative throughout the period, returned to deeply negative levels by the end of 2011.

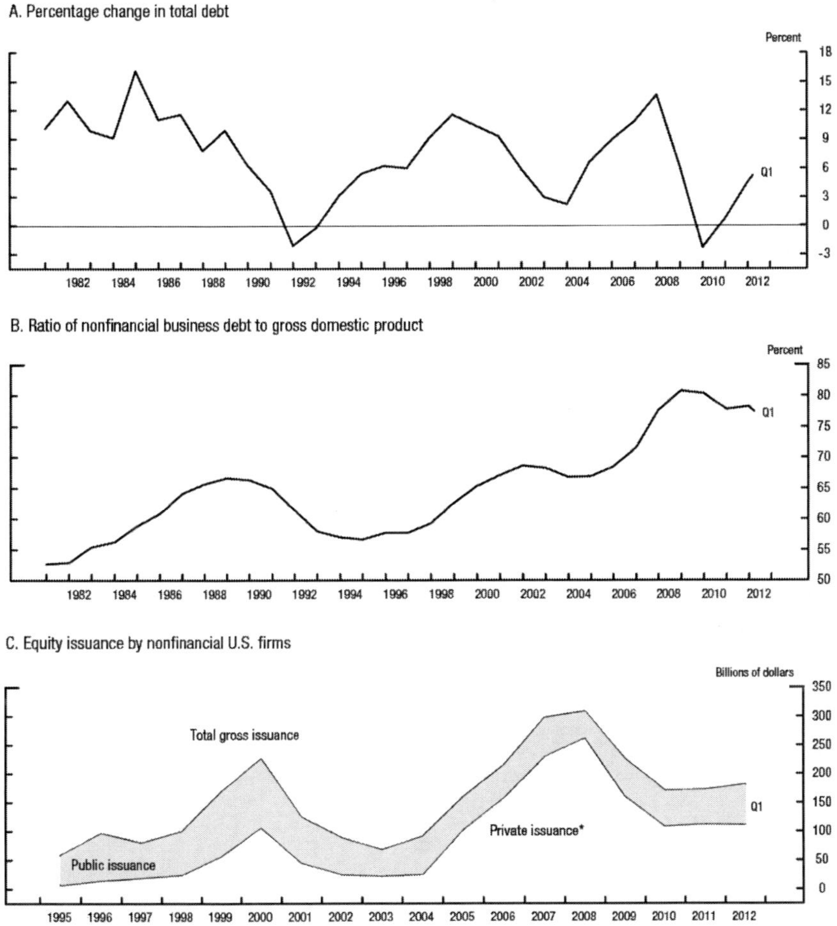

Note: Data are annual.

* Includes venture capital, buyouts, corporate finance, mezzanine, and other private equity investments.

Source: For panels A and B, Federal Reserve Board, flow of funds accounts; for panel C, Securities Data Company, the Private Equity Analyst, and the PricewaterhouseCoopers National Venture Capital Association Money Tree Report.

Figure 1. Total debt and equity of nonfinancial businesses, 1980–2012.

Financing by Nonfinancial Corporations

The financial crisis left a heavy imprint on the financing conditions for firms in public capital markets and at banks. Default rates on corporate bonds and on commercial and industrial (C&I) loans, which had fallen to near-historical lows in 2006 and 2007, rose sharply starting in late 2008 but retraced most of their increases after 2009 (figure 2, panel A). Yields on BBB-rated and high-yield corporate bonds soared during the height of the financial crisis in late 2008 and early 2009 but fell to almost record lows in the subsequent years (figure 2, panel B). The spreads of yields on corporate bonds to those on comparable-maturity Treasury securities also rose steeply during the height of the financial crisis but declined over 2009 and have since remained a bit above pre-recession levels (figure 2, panel C). Borrowing costs for shorter-term debt issued by nonfinancial firms also increased substantially during the financial crisis. In particular, rates on commercial paper issued by A2/P2-rated nonfinancial corporations increased sharply in 2008 but dropped in 2009 and have remained very low since then (figure 2, panel D). Similarly, the spreads of rates on A2/P2-rated commercial paper over the target federal funds rate moved up in 2007, skyrocketed in 2008, and retraced most of their increases in 2009 (figure 2, panel E).

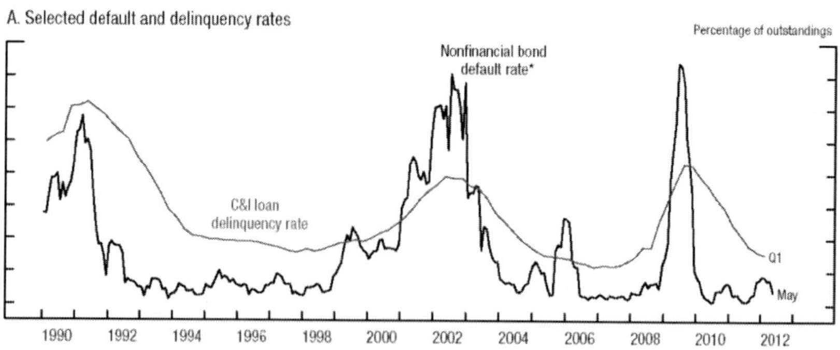

Note: C&I is commercial and industrial.

* Six-month trailing defaults divided by beginning-of-period outstandings, at an annual rate.

Source: For default rate, Moody's Investors Service; for delinquency rate, Call Report data.

Figure 2. Continued

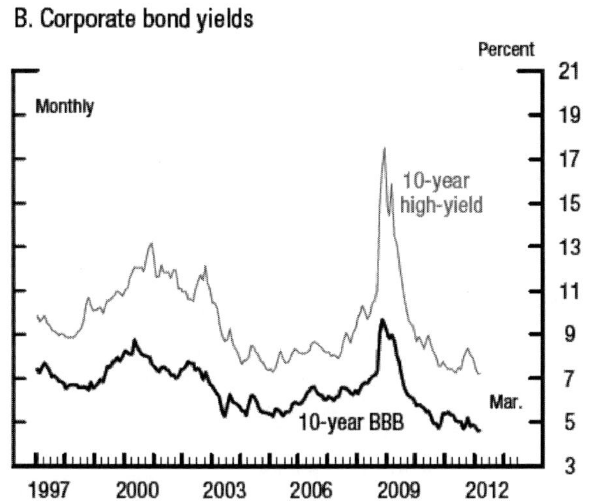

Source: Federal Reserve Board staff estimates of smoothed yield curves based on Merrill Lynch bond data.

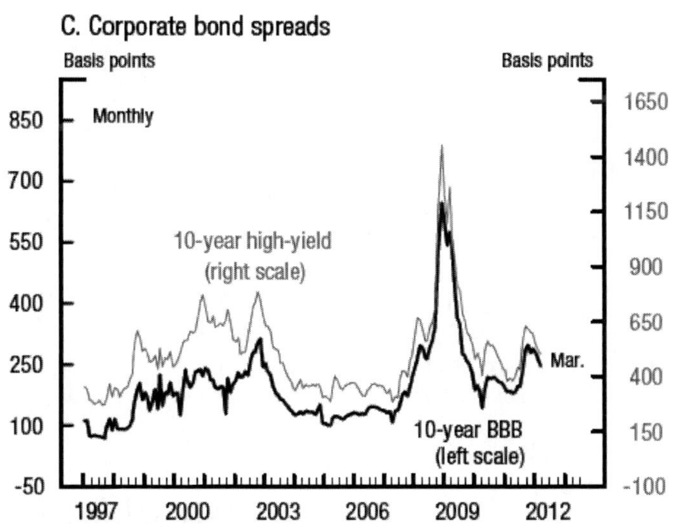

Note: Spreads over 10-year Treasury yield.

Source: Federal Reserve Board staff estimates of smoothed corporate yield curves based on Merrill Lynch data and smoothed Treasury yield curve.

Figure 2. (Continued)

D. Commercial paper yields

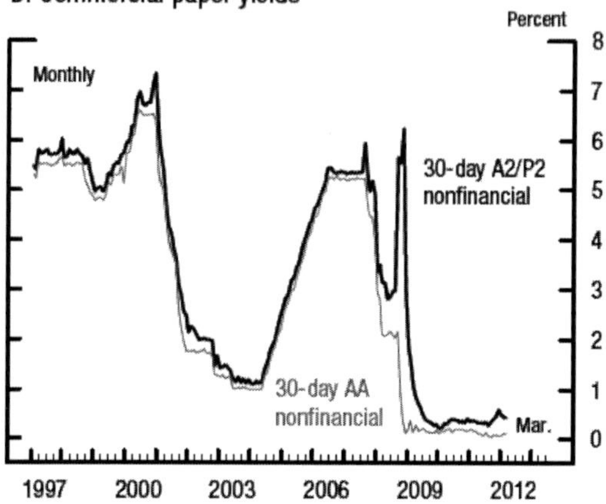

Source: Depository Trust & Clearing Corporation.

E. Commercial paper spreads

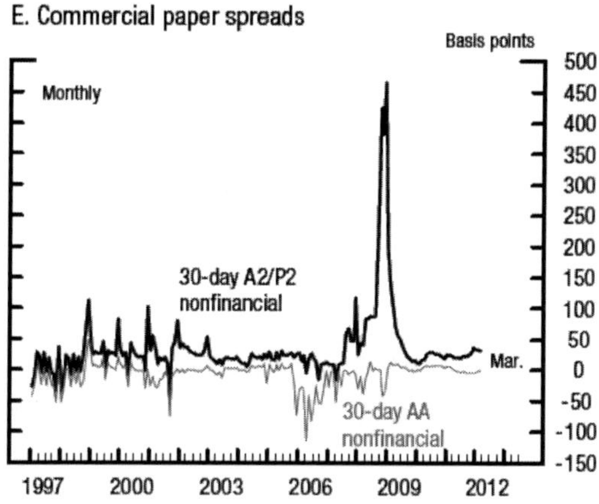

Note: Spreads computed over the target federal funds rate.
Source: For commercial paper, Depository Trust & Clearing Corporation.

Figure 2. Corporate credit conditions, 1990–2012.

Nonfinancial corporate debt rose in 2007 and early 2008 and then contracted sharply during the height of the financial crisis, but it has expanded at a moderate pace since 2010 (figure 3). The pace of bond issuance by nonfinancial corporations, while still positive, declined sharply in the second half of 2008, but it picked up notably over the next two years, reflecting in part falling yields on corporate bonds. Commercial paper outstanding at nonfinancial firms dropped sharply in 2009 but rebounded over the next two years. In contrast, loans from banks contracted in 2009 and 2010 but have increased since then. As a result of tight lending standards and depressed real estate prices, commercial mortgage debt has declined steadily since 2007.

Level of debt, 2007–12 Billions of dollars						
Type of debt	**2007**	**2008**	**2009**	**2010**	**2011**	**2012:Q1**
Total debt	6,760	7,036	6,784	7,051	7,534	7,651
Bonds[1]	3,676	3,881	4,269	4,691	5,077	5,193
Mortgages	929	878	758	690	623	615
Bank loans[2]	716	780	560	545	619	612
Commercial paper	124	131	58	83	116	128
Other loans[3]	1,316	1,365	1,139	1,041	1,100	1,105
MEMO						
Trade debt	1,898	1,673	1,587	1,751	1,935	1,969

Note: Debt outstanding at end of period. Seasonally adjusted data.

[1] Industrial revenue bonds and corporate bonds.

[2] Extended without real estate as collateral.

[3] Loans from finance companies and all other nonmortgage loans that are not extended by banks.

Source: Federal Reserve Board, flow of funds accounts.

Growth rates of bank loans and total debt for nonfinancial corporate businesses, 1980–2012

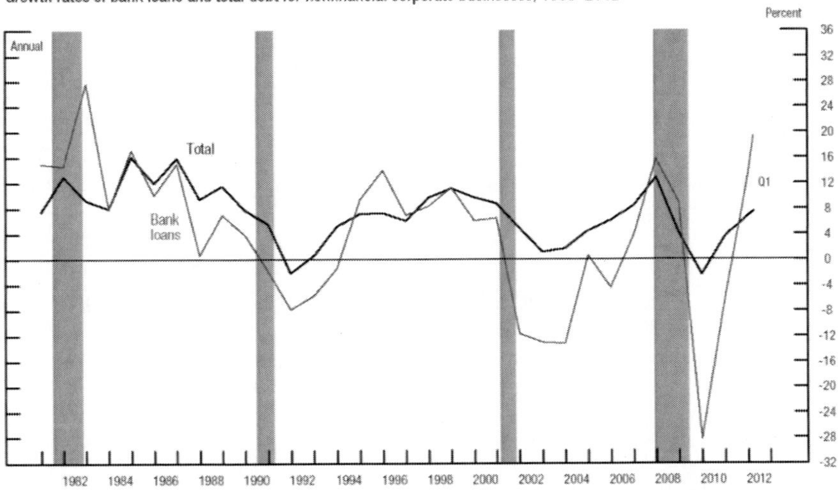

Note: The shaded bars indicate periods of business recession as defined by the National Bureau of Economic Research.

Source: Federal Reserve Board, flow of funds accounts.

Figure 3. Total debt of nonfinancial corporate businesses.

Table 1. Small business loan and microloan holdings of U.S. commercial banking organizations, by type of loan, 2007–11

Size of loan and year	All	Commercial and industrial	Nonfarm nonresidential real estate
Small business loans ($1 million or less)			
Amount outstanding, June 30 (billions of dollars)			
2007	595.8	275.5	320.4
2008	616.1	286.4	329.7
2009	604.2	274.0	330.2
2010	568.9	266.2	302.8
2011	529.7	241.4	288.3
Change[1] (percent)			
2008	3.4	4.0	2.9
2009	-1.9	-4.3	.2
2010	-5.8	-2.9	-8.3
2011	-6.9	-9.3	-4.8
Microloans ($100,000 or less)			
Amount outstanding, June 30 (billions of dollars)			
2007	124.4	99.1	25.3
2008	136.7	111.9	24.8
2009	128.5	104.5	24.0
2010	130.5	110.5	20.0
2011	111.2	93.3	17.9
Change[1] (percent)			
2008	9.9	12.9	-1.9
2009	-6.0	-6.7	-3.1
2010	1.6	5.8	-16.6
2011	-14.8	-15.6	-10.7

Note: Small business loans are business loans of $1 million or less; microloans, a subset of small business loans, are for $100,000 or less. U.S. commercial banking organizations are insured U.S. domestically chartered banks excluding credit card institutions and U.S. branches and agencies of foreign banks. Details many not sum to totals because of rounding.

[1] Change is measured from June of the preceding year to June of the year indicated.

Source: Call Reports (June 30), various years.

Financing by Small Businesses

Fully comprehensive data that directly measure the financing activities of small businesses do not exist. However, various sources of information can serve as proxies for small business activity and can be used to identify patterns of small business financing. These sources suggest that financing flows to small businesses weakened considerably as a result of the financial crisis and the recession, and that they have only partly recovered.

Total small business debt outstanding, estimated as the total debt of partnerships and proprietorships, increased in 2007 and for most of 2008, but it dropped from 2009 through the first half of 2011 (figure 4).[10] Since then, small business debt has rebounded a bit, though at a moderate pace relative to other recent recessions. The two largest components of total small business debt are mortgage debt and loans not secured by real estate that are made by commercial banks. Bank loans extended without real estate collateral have followed a pattern similar to that of total partnerships and proprietorships debt, falling during the financial crisis but recovering somewhat in the second half of 2011. In contrast, mortgage debt has declined since 2009 as a result of the general weakness in real estate markets. Commercial bank loans (both with and without real estate collateral) with principal less than or equal to $1 million, which are often extended to small firms, have also shown declines through the first half of 2011 (table 1).

Indicators of small business financing needs suggest that demand for credit started to decline around 2006, plummeted in 2008, and has shown signs of recovery since 2010. The demand for small business financing can be inferred from small business investment plans as reported in surveys conducted by the National Federation of Independent Business (NFIB).[11] According to the surveys, the net percentage of firms that planned capital outlays and the net percentage that anticipated business expansions were at about their historical averages in 2005 and 2006, plummeted to record lows during the financial crisis, and have increased only slightly in recent years (figure 5). Data on demand for C&I loans, as reported in the Federal Reserve Board's Senior Loan Officer Opinion Survey on Bank Lending Practices (SLOOS), show a similar decline during the financial crisis but suggest a somewhat stronger recovery after the recession.[12]

Credit conditions for small business lending by banks became substantially tighter during the financial crisis but have eased notably since 2010. Results from the SLOOS indicate that lending standards for small borrowers tightened substantially in 2008 and 2009 but loosened in 2010 and 2011 (figure 6). The net percentage of NFIB respondents reporting that credit had become more difficult to obtain, which had remained low by historical standards in the years prior to the financial crisis, rose in 2008 and reached its highest levels on record in 2009. Since then, it has retraced a good portion of its increases during the financial crisis, as the average short-term interest rate paid by NFIB respondents decreased from about 9 percent in 2007 to about 6 percent in the first quarter of 2012.[13] Although credit conditions for small firms tightened notably during the financial crisis, responses to other questions in the NFIB survey suggest that small business owners have remained cautious. In particular, since 2008, respondents have appeared to remain more concerned about their outlook for sales than about credit conditions, as most cite weak product demand as the most significant problem they face.

Level of debt, 2007–12
Billions of dollars

Type of debt	2007	2008	2009	2010	2011	2012:Q1
Total debt	3,775	4,093	3,959	3,762	3,773	3,784
Mortgages	2,593	2,764	2,755	2,621	2,585	2,569
Bank loans[1]	882	1,000	884	815	866	895
Other loans[2]	165	177	172	177	177	178
MEMO						
Trade debt	379	367	370	355	356	357

Note: Debt outstanding at end of period.

[1] Extended without real estate as collateral.

[2] Loans from finance companies and all other nonmortgage loans that are not extended by banks.

Source: Federal Reserve Board, flow of funds accounts.

Growth rates of bank loans and total debt for partnerships and proprietorships, 1980–2012

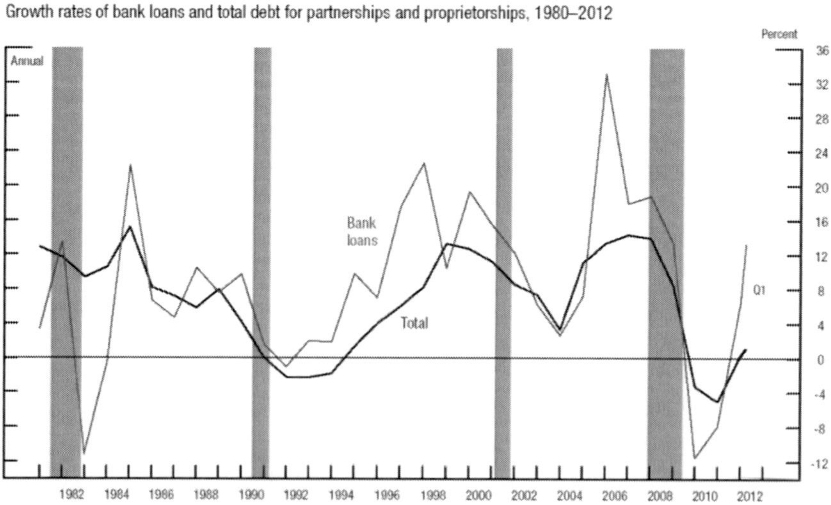

Note: The shaded bars indicate periods of business recession as defined by the National Bureau of Economic Research.

Source: Federal Reserve Board, flow of funds accounts.

Figure 4. Total debt of partnerships and proprietorships.

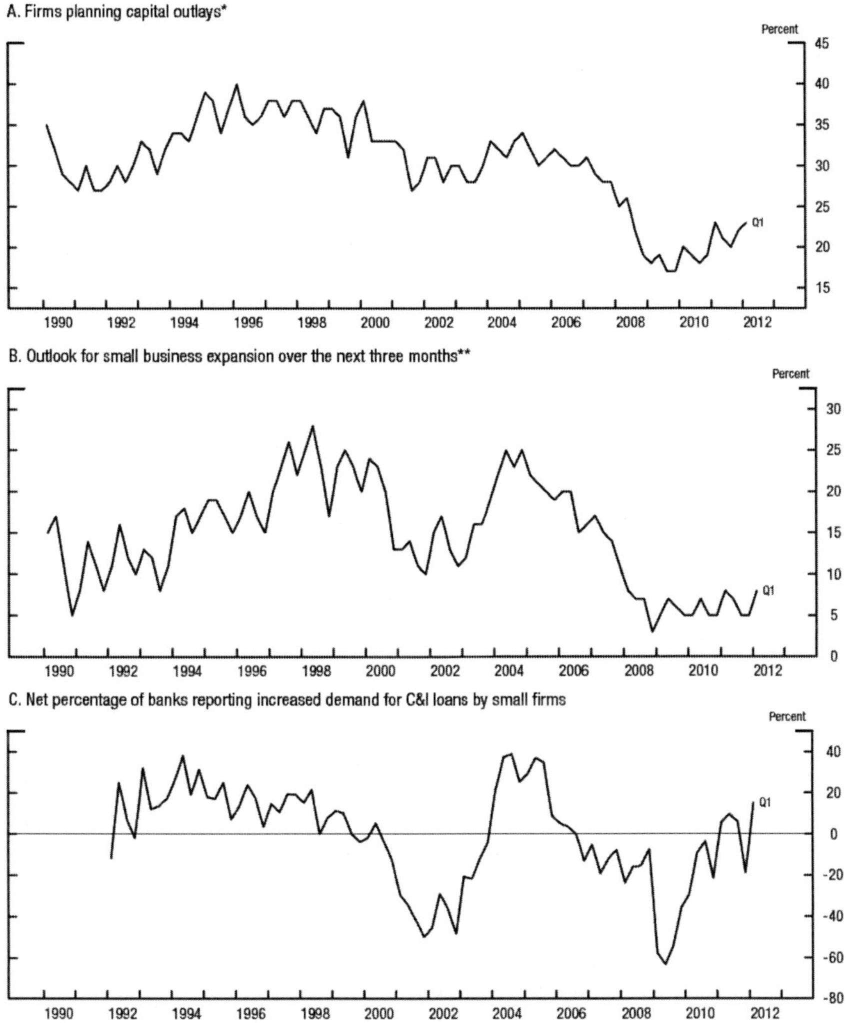

Note: Data are quarterly and not seasonally adjusted. In panel C, data start in 1992. C&I is commercial and industrial.

* Percentage of firms planning capital outlays in the next six months.

** Percentage of firms that consider the next three months a good time to expand.

Source: For panels A and B, National Federation of Independent Business; for panel C, Federal Reserve Board, Senior Loan Officer Opinion Survey on Bank Lending Practices.

Figure 5. Demand for small business credit, 1990–2012.

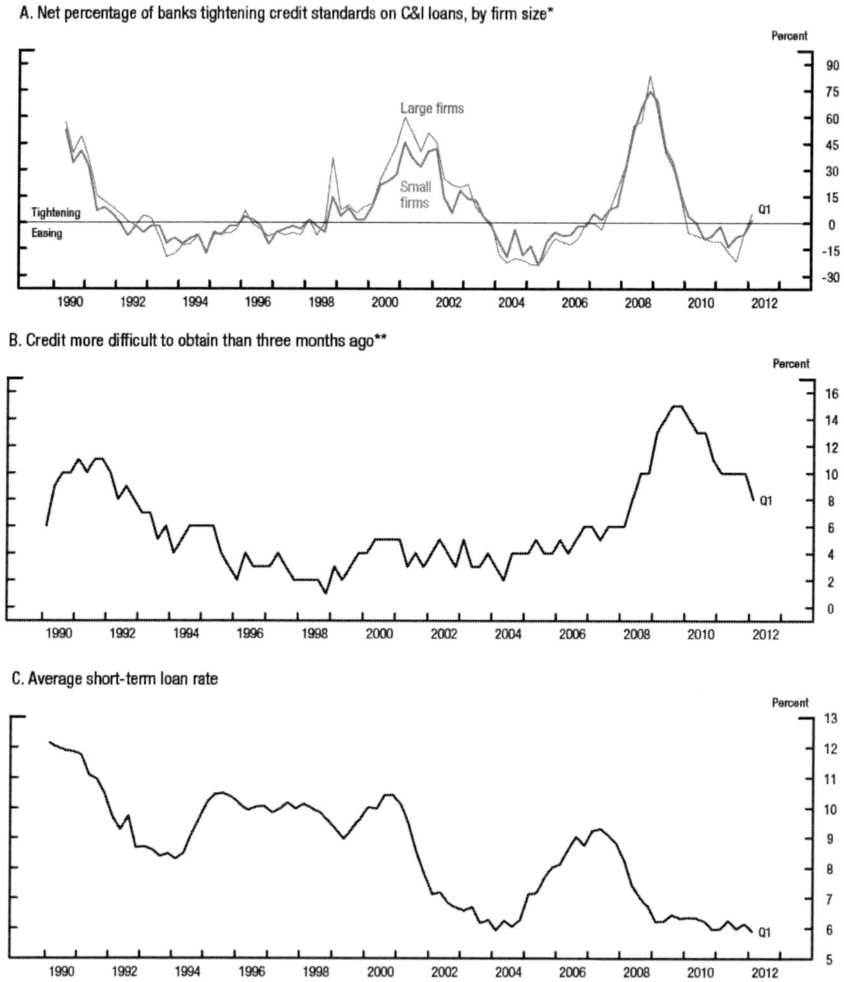

Note: Data are quarterly and not seasonally adjusted. C&I is commercial and industrial.

* Firms with annual sales of more than $50 million are considered large.

** Of borrowers who sought credit in the past three months, the proportion that reported difficulty in obtaining credit less the proportion that reported more ease in obtaining credit.

Source: For panel A, Federal Reserve Board, Senior Loan Officer Opinion Survey on Bank Lending Practices; for panels B and C, National Federation of Independent Business.

Figure 6. Credit availability to small businesses, 1990–2012.

CREDIT USE BY SMALL BUSINESSES

This section examines the composition and borrowing behavior of small firms to identify characteristics that are associated with important patterns of credit use. It also discusses the special role that small business plays in the U.S. economy and the unique challenges small firms face in obtaining credit.

Small Business: Definition and Background

Defining what is meant by "small business" is the difficult first step in conducting a policy-relevant analysis of the financing needs of small business. The financing needs are very different for a "mom and pop" grocery store, a microenterprise in the inner city, a start-up high-tech firm, a business that is ready to expand from early-stage growth to the next higher level, or a business that has neared the point of issuing public debt or equity. Yet the term "small business" encompasses all of these entities. According to a broad guideline used by the U.S. Small Business Administration (SBA), a small business is a firm or enterprise with fewer than 500 employees. This definition encompasses nearly all businesses in the United States.

The U.S. Census Bureau's County Business Patterns data indicate that there were over 7.4 million active employer establishments in March 2009.[14] The vast majority of these establishments were modest in size, with more than one-half of them employing fewer than 5 employees and nearly an additional one-third employing between 5 and 19 employees. In total, small employer establishments with fewer than 500 employees constituted 99.8 percent of all employer businesses, a fraction that is consistent with previous years (table 2).

More than one-third of small employer establishments were organized as S corporations (37.7 percent), and just under an additional one-third as C corporations (31.1 percent). The primary difference between the two types of corporations is that C corporations are subject to corporate income tax, while S corporations are not. However, S corporations are legally constrained to have no more than 75 shareholders; are restricted to one class of stock; and, to avoid income tax liability, must pass all income to the owners at the end of each fiscal year. The remaining small employer establishments were organized as sole proprietorships (13.3 percent), partnerships (10.1 percent), and nonprofits (7.5 percent).

Table 2. Characteristics of small employer firms, 2009

Characteristic	Establishments	Employment	First-quarter payroll
Percent			
Employment (number of employees)			
1–4	54.8	7.7	6.5
5–9	18.9	10.2	8.5
10–19	12.8	14.0	12.2
20–49	8.6	21.0	19.6
50–99	2.9	16.1	16.4
100–249	1.6	19.7	22.1
250–499	.4	11.3	14.8
Legal form of organization			
C corporation	31.1	45.4	53.9
Individual proprietorship	13.3	4.5	2.9
Partnership	10.1	10.8	10.5
S corporation	37.7	28.5	24.2
Nonprofit	7.5	9.9	7.6
Government	.0	.2	.2
Other legal forms of organization	.3	.4	.4
Industry			
Agriculture, forestry, and fishing and hunting	.3	.2	.1
Mining, quarrying, and oil and gas extraction	.4	.5	.9
Utilities	.2	.5	1.2
Construction	9.6	6.0	6.7
Manufacturing	4.1	9.3	10.3
Wholesale trade	5.7	5.7	7.9
Retail trade	14.5	15.8	9.4
Transportation and warehousing	2.8	3.3	3.2
Information	1.8	2.6	4.6
Finance and insurance	6.6	5.0	10.7
Real estate and rental and leasing	4.7	2.1	2.1
Professional, scientific, and technical services	11.3	7.0	11.3
Management of companies and enterprises	.7	1.8	4.6

Characteristic	Establishments	Employment	First-quarter payroll
Administrative and support and waste management and remediation services	5.1	6.3	4.9
Educational services	1.2	1.8	1.4
Health care and social assistance	10.7	12.9	11.4
Arts, entertainment, and recreation	1.7	1.8	1.2
Accommodation and food services	8.6	11.8	4.3
Other services (except public administration)	9.7	5.5	3.6
Industries not classified	.2	.0	.0
Census region			
Northeast	19.3	18.8	22.0
Midwest	21.9	23.2	21.4
South	35.1	35.7	33.6
West	23.7	22.3	23.0

Source: Statistics calculated based on 2009 County Business Patterns data from the U.S. Census Bureau, www.census.gov/econ/cbp.

Small businesses operate in every major segment of the U.S. economy. The most common industry for small employer establishments in 2009 was retail trade, which accounted for 1 out of 7 small firms. About one-half of establishments were in construction, health care and social assistance, professional and technical services, accommodation and food services, and other services, each of which accounted for roughly one-tenth of small employer establishments. The remaining small establishments were principally involved in finance and insurance (6.6 percent), wholesale trade (5.7 percent), administrative support (5.1 percent), real estate and leasing (4.7 percent), manufacturing (4.1 percent), and transportation and warehousing (2.8 percent).

Geographically, small establishments were widely dispersed throughout the nation, with 19.3 percent operating in the Northeast, 21.9 percent in the Midwest, 23.7 percent in the West, and the remaining 35.1 percent in the South. This distribution roughly reflects the 2009 population distribution, with 18.0 percent of the population living in the Northeast, 21.8 percent in the Midwest, 23.3 percent in the West, and the remaining 36.9 percent in the South (U.S. Census Bureau, Population Division, 2009).

Small businesses contribute significantly to the strength and vigor of the U.S. economy. Establishments with fewer than 500 employees accounted for nearly 80 percent of total covered sector employment and over 70 percent of first-quarter payroll.[15] In addition, most large and successful companies begin as smaller firms that prosper and grow.

The concerns of the Congress and other policymaking bodies about small business financing largely stem from the perception that small firms have more difficulty gaining access to credit sources than do large businesses or other types of borrowers. The source of this difficulty may be the greater riskiness of small firms and the associated high costs of evaluating and monitoring credit risks, or it may be inefficiencies in markets that hinder pricing of risk or impede the effective pooling of risks. To the extent that private-market impediments or inefficiencies are the source of any difficulties for small business financing, policymakers may focus on measures that address these factors. In this case, no one policy prescription would likely work for all, and no one definition of small business would be appropriate. As discussed in this chapter, credit needs and borrowing sources differ widely among small businesses.

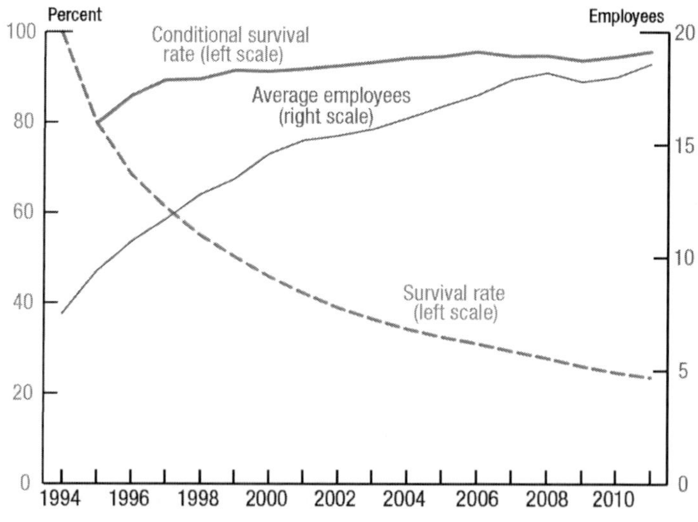

Note: The data for the conditional survival rate start in 1995.
Source: Bureau of Labor Statistics, Business Employment Dynamics data.

Figure 7. Survival, conditional survival, and average employment among establishments born in 1994, 1994–2011.

Risks of Lending to Small Businesses

Lending to small businesses is generally considered riskier and more costly than lending to larger firms. Business Employment Dynamics data, compiled by the Bureau of Labor Statistics, provide insights into some of the risks. Figure 7 depicts the survival and conditional survival rates as well as the average employment for a cohort of employer firms that were born in 1994.[16] Because a cohort is restricted to the fixed group of firms initially included, the survival rate—the share of all firms that began in 1994 and are still in business in each subsequent year must decline over time as firms go out of business. In contrast, the conditional survival 2011 rate the share of firms that were in business in the previous year and continue operations in the current year may rise or fall each year. The average employment is calculated among firms in business in each year. It, too, may rise or fall over time.

Two facets of small business dynamics can be observed in figure 7. First, the increasing average size among the surviving businesses indicates that small businesses are more apt to fail in any given year of existence than larger or growing ones. Second, the failure rate in the early years when the firm is likely to be the smallest is quite high relative to later years. For example, 20 percent of establishments born in 1994 failed in the first year (by 1995), but only 11 percent failed in the second. Conditional on having survived the first three years in business, more than 90 percent of establishments will continue to be in business the following year. Historically, and particularly in the early life of a business, lenders have had difficulty determining the creditworthiness of applicants for small business loans. The heterogeneity across small firms, together with widely varying uses of borrowed funds, has impeded the development of general standards for assessing applications for small business loans and has made evaluating such loans relatively expensive.

Lending to small businesses is further complicated by the "informational opacity" of many such firms. Obtaining reliable information on the creditworthiness of a small business is often difficult because little, if any, public information exists about the performance of most small businesses. Small businesses rarely have publicly traded equity or debt securities, and public information on such firms is typically sparse. Many small businesses also lack detailed balance sheets and other financial information often used by lenders in making underwriting decisions.

The cost to the lender does not end with the decision to grant a loan. Small business lenders typically have had to monitor the credit arrangement with individual borrowers. For very small firms, a close association between the finances of the business and those of the owner may increase loan-monitoring costs.

Historically, the relatively elevated costs of evaluating small business applications and the ongoing costs of monitoring firm performance have made loans to small businesses less attractive for some lenders, especially because, when expressed as a percentage of the (small) dollar amount of the proposed loan, these noninterest costs are often quite high compared with loans to middle-market or large corporate borrowers. Financial institutions, especially commercial banks, are believed to have an advantage in dealing with information problems. Through interactions with a firm that uses its financial services, the lending institution can obtain additional information about the firm's activities, ownership, financial characteristics, and prospects that are important in deciding whether to extend credit.[17] Lenders can use information gathered over time through longterm relationships with business owners and other members of the local community to monitor the health of the business and to build appropriate incentives into loan agreements.[18] The role of relationship lending will likely continue to be significant, even as developments such as automated banking, credit scoring, and bank consolidation influence the competitive structure of the banking industry.[19]

Insights on the risks of lending to small businesses may be gained by examining delinquency rates at banks that primarily do small business lending, small-business-lending-intensive (SBLI) banks. During the recent financial crisis and ensuing recession, these risks became much more obvious as small businesses struggled to keep current on their outstanding debt. Figure 8 shows the delinquency rates for C&I and commercial real estate (CRE) loans for SBLI banks compared with other banks.[20] In the early part of the decade, delinquency rates at these SBLI banks were similar to such rates at other banks for C&I loans. However, in 2007, delinquency rates at SBLI banks began to rise for C&I loans faster than delinquency rates at other banks. The rate peaked at nearly 7 percent in 2009 at SBLI banks, compared with about 4 percent at other banks. Since then, the rate has come down but remains elevated and above the rate at other banks. For CRE loans, the story was slightly different. Until 2009, the delinquency rate at SBLI banks was slightly above the delinquency rate at other banks. In 2011, the delinquency rate at SBLI banks peaked slightly below the rate at other banks but continues to be considerably higher than pre-recession levels.

Credit Use

Up-to-date and comprehensive information about the universe of small businesses is sparse, and most evidence about financing needs and sources is derived from surveys. In light of this reality, the NFIB sponsored surveys in 2009, 2010, and 2011 to gauge the credit access of small firms during the financial crisis and ensuing economic turmoil.

Each of the three NFIB samples was drawn from the Dun & Bradstreet Market Identifier File and included between 750 and 850 small employer firms. For the surveys, small employer firms were defined as firms with between 1 and 250 employees in addition to the owner(s). The samples were stratified by employment size, and weighted responses are representative of the Dun & Bradstreet population of small employer firms in the United States in 2009, 2010, and 2011.[21]

These three surveys quantify the use of and access to credit by small employer firms in the 12 months prior to each survey.[22] Respondents were asked to provide information about their applications for and current use of four distinct types of credit: new credit lines, renewal of existing credit lines, business loans from financial institutions, and credit cards (including personal cards used for business purposes). Small business owners were also asked about their real estate holdings and whether those properties are used by the business as collateral for business borrowing.

Data from the NFIB surveys describe patterns of credit use by small businesses. Although credit use is ultimately the intersection of demand and supply factors, it is nonetheless very useful in developing a picture of the demand for credit by small businesses. The data reveal patterns at both the aggregate and firm levels. It is important to keep in mind that the surveys are not following the same firms in each year, so it is not possible to say what happened to the credit demand and use of a *particular* firm over time, but it is possible to say what happened to the credit demand and use of a representative *sample* of small firms over time.[23]

Types of Credit Used

Small businesses use a variety of types of credit to fulfill their financial needs, including loans taken down under lines of credit, other term loans, trade credit, and credit cards. Patterns for each product are discussed here.

A. C&I loans 30 or more days delinquent and nonaccruing loans

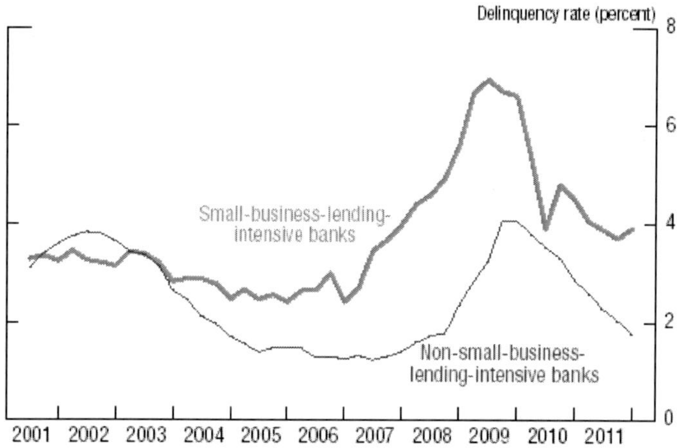

B. CRE loans 30 or more days delinquent and nonaccruing loans

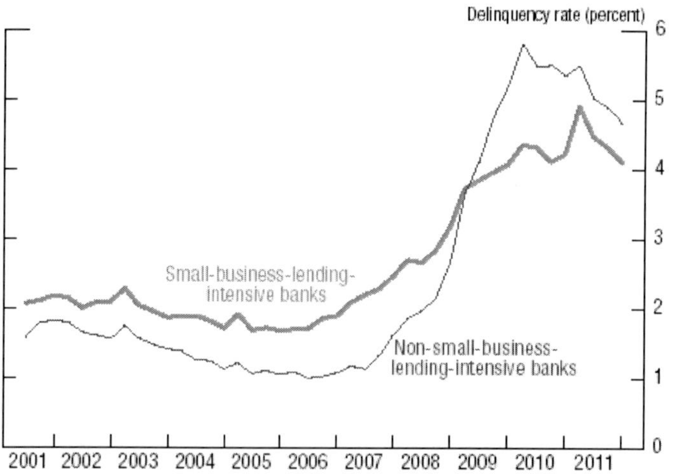

Note: Small-business-lending-intensive banks are defined as institutions where 80 percent or more of their commercial and industrial (C&I) and commercial real estate (CRE) loans have initial values of $1 million or less.

Source: The data are constructed from special tabulations of Call Reports (Consolidated Reports of Condition and Income for U.S. Banks, Schedule RC-C, Part II: Loans to Small Businesses and Small Farms) dated June 30, 2001, to December 31, 2011.

Figure 8. Delinquency rates at commercial banks, 2001–11.

Credit Lines

Credit lines were more commonly used than term loans by small businesses in each year, with just under one-half of firms reporting having such a line (table 3). Between 2009 and 2011, the fraction of firms with lines of credit varied little. Among firms with at least one line of credit, the median firm had a single line. The average number of lines per firm steadily increased from 1.4 in 2009 to 1.7 in 2011.

Substantial variation exists in the use of credit lines by size of firm. Roughly one-third of the firms with fewer than two employees reported using a line of credit in each year, compared with two-thirds of firms with at least 50 employees. The usage pattern by size holds up over time, but usage rates are a bit higher in 2010 than in either 2009 or 2011.

The usage pattern by age of firm is less clear. In general, usage seems to increase until the firm reaches 10 to 20 years old, and then holds steady or drops off slightly. Between 2009 and 2011, an increasing fraction of older firms had lines of credit. For example, 48.4 percent of firms 30 or more years old had a line of credit in 2009, while 64.6 percent of them did so in 2011. The same is not true of the youngest firms, whose usage peaked in 2010. For all but the oldest firms, the average number of lines was highest in 2011 among firms with at least one line of credit.

Credit line usage by industry over this period reveals no obvious pattern. In 2009, firms in "other" industries were most likely to use lines of credit, with nearly 6 out of 10 such firms reporting having at least one line of credit. This fraction falls over time to 4 out of 10 in 2011. The next most frequent users in 2009 were construction and manufacturing firms, with one-half of firms in both industries reporting having lines of credit. However, their paths go in opposite directions over time. While an increasing fraction of manufacturing firms report lines of credit in 2010 and 2011, the opposite is true of construction firms. This divergence is likely partially attributable to difficulties in the housing market, which employs a fair share of small construction firms. Five out of 10 firms in professional services and 4 out of 10 firms in nonprofessional services report having lines of credit in 2009. Over time, increasing fractions of firms in professional services and decreasing fractions of firms in nonprofessional services report having lines of credit. Over two-fifths of firms in wholesale and retail trade and one-third of firms in finance and real estate have lines of credit in 2009; in 2011, one-half of firms in wholesale and retail trade and two-fifths of firms in finance and real estate have them.

Table 3. Use of credit lines, 2009–11

Category of firm	2009			2010			2011		
	Percent that use a credit line	Number of firms with lines among a credit line		Percent that use a credit line	Number of firms with lines among a credit line		Percent that use a credit line	Number of lines among firms with a credit line	
		Mean	Median		Mean	Median		Mean	Median
All firms	**45.6**	**1.4**	**1**	**46.8**	**1.5**	**1**	**45.4**	**1.7**	**1**
Number of employees									
0–1	33.8	1.5	1	39.0	1.3	1	33.7	1.9	1
2–4	39.6	1.2	1	43.5	1.4	1	43.7	1.5	1
5–9	53.5	1.6	1	42.4	1.8	1	56.3	2.3	1
10–19	57.3	1.7	1	59.3	1.5	1	44.1	1.4	1
20–49	66.0	1.5	1	68.6	1.6	1	56.7	1.5	1
50–250	71.2	1.6	1	76.6	1.6	1	65.4	1.8	1
Age groups (years)									
Less than 4	30.6	1.4	1	37.5	1.6	1	26.0	1.8	1
4–6	41.8	1.4	1	30.4	1.2	1	47.3	1.4	1
7–9	46.7	1.4	1	42.2	1.3	1	53.1	2.1	1
10–14	51.7	1.6	1	50.8	1.4	1	38.0	2.4	1
15–19	48.0	1.5	1	53.0	1.6	1	59.2	1.7	1
20–29	46.6	1.4	1	51.4	1.5	1	53.2	1.8	1
30 or more	48.4	1.4	1	49.0	1.6	1	64.6	1.4	1
Industry									
Construction and mining	51.6	1.5	1	47.1	1.7	1	45.5	2.5	1
Manufacturing	51.6	1.3	1	51.8	1.2	1	63.6	1.1	1
Wholesale/retail trade	44.3	1.5	1	51.6	1.4	1	49.9	1.5	1
Finance/real estate	33.0	1.3	1	43.3	1.7	1	39.6	2.8	1
Nonprofessional services	41.1	1.4	1	41.6	1.5	1	35.4	1.8	1
Professional services	49.0	1.6	1	47.5	1.4	1	53.0	1.3	1
Other	58.1	1.4	1	44.8	1.6	1	41.1	1.4	1

Note: Data are representative of small employer firms with 1 to 250 employees in addition to the owner(s) in the year of the survey.

Source: National Federation of Independent Business, annual finance surveys of 2009, 2010, and 2011.

The surveys do not provide information on either the size of the line of credit or the amount by which the line has been taken down.

Business Loans

Business loan usage trended down between 2009 and 2011. In 2009, nearly 36 percent of small employer firms reported that they had at least one business loan; in 2011, less than 30 percent of such firms so reported (table 4). This overall trend is not consistent when looking at firms according to size, age, and industry.

The more employees a firm has, the more likely it is to have at least one business loan. For example, in 2009, roughly 1 in 5 of the smallest firms reported having a business loan, compared with nearly 1 in 2 of the largest firms. The number of loans also varied substantially, with the number generally increasing with the size of the firm. Over the recent period, business loans generally became less common among the smallest firms and more common among the largest firms.

By age, there is roughly an inverted-U-shaped pattern, with use being lowest among the youngest firms, increasing as firms age, and dropping off among the oldest firms. As firms age and grow, the need for business loans may increase, which may reflect a life-cycle growth pattern; once firms get to a certain age, most have reached their optimal size and have less need for loans to grow and expand. Over the recent period, usage rates fluctuated significantly by age of firm. For example, 20.4 percent of the youngest firms reported having a business loan in 2009; this proportion increased to 36.2 percent in 2010 and then fell to 14.5 percent in 2011. In contrast, 32.1 percent of firms aged 15 to 19 reported having a business loan in 2009; this proportion increased to 41.5 percent in 2010 and then fell back some to 37.7 percent in 2011.

Business loan usage varies substantially by industry. In 2009, business loan usage was lowest among firms in professional services (26.7 percent) and highest among firms in manufacturing (55.4 percent). While usage remained fairly constant for firms in professional services, the share of manufacturing firms using business loans decreased markedly from 2009 to 2011, with only 29.2 percent of manufacturing firms reporting having a business loan in 2011. Although not as large as the decline among manufacturing firms, a decrease in the share of firms in construction and nonprofessional services that reported having business loans between 2009 and 2011 was also observed.

Table 4. Use of business loans, 2009–11

Category of firm	2009			2010			2011		
	Percent that use a business loan	Number of loans among firms with a business loan		Percent that use a business loan	Number of loans among firms with a business loan		Percent that use a business loan	Number of loans among firms with a business loan	
		Mean	Median		Mean	Median		Mean	Median
All firms	**35.9**	**1.9**	**1**	**31.4**	**2.0**	**1**	**29.1**	**2.0**	**1**
Number of employees									
0–1	21.6	1.8	1	13.0	1.7	1	15.7	1.8	2
2–4	34.3	1.6	1	32.6	1.4	1	23.4	1.6	1
5–9	45.1	1.9	1	34.5	2.5	2	36.6	2.5	1
10–19	45.3	2.4	2	41.9	2.1	1	42.0	1.8	1
20–49	45.9	1.9	1	49.4	2.6	2	51.0	2.2	2
50–250	48.0	4.6	3	51.3	3.0	2	56.8	3.0	2
Age groups (years)									
Less than 4	20.4	1.6	1	36.2	1.4	1	14.5	1.5	1
4–6	34.7	1.5	1	23.8	1.8	1	25.9	1.9	1
7–9	38.2	1.8	1	26.9	2.5	2	39.6	1.9	1
10–14	39.9	1.8	1	36.2	1.9	1	35.8	2.6	1
15–19	32.1	2.9	2	41.5	1.6	1	37.7	2.2	1
20–29	44.4	1.9	1	29.2	1.9	2	32.0	2.0	2
30 or more	36.3	2.2	2	29.4	2.5	1	37.8	2.2	1
Industry									
Construction and mining	38.2	3.2	1	36.8	1.9	1	30.8	2.5	2
Manufacturing	55.4	2.3	2	45.8	1.7	1	29.2	2.9	2
Wholesale/retail trade	30.1	1.6	1	30.1	1.6	1	28.8	1.6	1
Finance/real estate	33.7	1.9	1	25.0	2.5	2	28.3	3.6	2
Nonprofessional services	39.8	1.6	1	37.6	1.9	1	27.8	1.9	1
Professional services	26.7	1.8	2	24.8	1.9	1	26.2	1.5	1
Other	40.0	1.8	1	26.7	3.1	2	35.3	1.9	2

Note: Data are representative of small employer firms with 1 to 250 employees in addition to the owner(s) in the year of the survey.

Source: National Federation of Independent Business, annual finance surveys of 2009, 2010, and 2011.

Alternatives to Traditional Credit

Small business owners may turn to alternative forms of credit if they find themselves unable to obtain traditional forms or if they find the terms of these other products more favorable. Two such alternatives credit cards and trade credit can be examined using data from the 2009 11 NFIB surveys. These widely used alternative forms of credit may be important both in financing small businesses and, as substitute products, in influencing the demand for traditional credit by small firms. According to the NFIB surveys, just under 60 percent of small firms used a credit line or business loan in each year, but just under 90 percent used a credit card or trade credit.

Credit Cards

Credit cards can serve as a convenient alternative to paying expenses by cash or check if a business pays balances on time and in full each month. They can also be a substitute for traditional forms of credit when balances are carried month to month. Survey evidence from earlier periods suggests that credit cards are used primarily for convenience.[24]

Credit cards used for business purposes can be issued to the firm itself (*business cards*) or to the owners of the firm (*personal cards*). Table 5 shows the percentage of small businesses that used personal credit cards, business credit cards, or either personal or business credit cards to pay for business expenses in 2009, 2010, and 2011.[25] The fraction of firms that use either a personal or business card declined somewhat over this period but remained near 80 percent in 2011. There seems to be a slight decline in the fraction using business cards and a slight increase in the fraction using personal cards. This decline in business card usage follows a period of rapid growth in business credit cards between 1998 and 2003.[26] In 2009, roughly one-fourth of personal credit card users and one-fifth of business credit card users actually used their cards as a source of credit. By 2011, nearly one-third of firms that used personal credit cards reported normally carrying a balance, while the share of firms using business credit cards and carrying a balance had not risen greatly.

The use of personal and business credit cards differed by size of firm. Business use of personal credit cards generally decreased as firm size increased, whereas the use of business credit cards increased with firm size. In 2009, only the smallest businesses used personal credit cards as often as business credit cards. This difference may indicate that small firms have more difficulty than larger firms in obtaining business credit cards and therefore use personal cards as a substitute.[27]

Table 5. Use of credit cards, 2009–11

Category of firm	2009 Percent that use a credit card, by type of card			2010 Percent that use a credit card, by type of card			2011 Percent that use a credit card, by type of card		
	Personal credit card for business purposes	Business credit card	Personal or business credit card	Personal credit card for business purposes	Business credit card	Personal or business credit card	Personal credit card for business purposes	Business credit card	Personal or business credit card
All firms	**40.3**	**63.8**	**82.7**	**39.7**	**57.5**	**76.1**	**43.5**	**58.8**	**79.1**
Share of card users that carry a balance	26.1	18.3	n.a.	24.8	22.6	n.a.	32.2	20.3	n.a.
Number of employees									
0–1	n.r.	n.r.	n.r.	42.9	42.9	70.1	44.9	55.1	77.5
2–4	n.r.	n.r.	n.r.	43.5	53.6	73.2	45.5	53.9	77.8
5–9	n.r.	n.r.	n.r.	34.5	66.9	80.6	45.8	66.2	83.1
10–19	n.r.	n.r.	n.r.	31.4	71.0	82.4	36.4	63.2	79.3
20–49	n.r.	n.r.	n.r.	34.6	73.5	84.5	39.7	66.0	79.2
50–250	n.r.	n.r.	n.r.	39.2	75.2	88.7	29.9	74.9	83.2
Age groups (years)									
Less than 4	n.r.	n.r.	n.r.	24.0	49.3	64.0	39.3	51.8	71.7
4–6	n.r.	n.r.	n.r.	25.5	59.1	72.7	44.1	60.0	78.2
7–9	n.r.	n.r.	n.r.	41.8	60.5	78.7	54.3	57.9	84.4
10–14	n.r.	n.r.	n.r.	43.4	54.3	76.1	38.2	63.7	83.4
15–19	n.r.	n.r.	n.r.	43.5	61.4	80.4	49.5	68.2	85.6
20–29	n.r.	n.r.	n.r.	43.3	56.2	78.6	49.3	56.7	85.5
30 or more	n.r.	n.r.	n.r.	43.0	62.9	77.3	39.7	61.8	76.7
Industry									
Construction and mining	n.r.	n.r.	n.r.	40.3	63.3	78.2	47.0	69.8	87.5
Manufacturing	n.r.	n.r.	n.r.	43.0	75.0	86.5	39.1	72.5	85.3
Wholesale/retail trade	n.r.	n.r.	n.r.	34.1	52.5	69.6	43.9	65.6	83.6
Finance/real estate	n.r.	n.r.	n.r.	44.6	69.6	84.6	33.6	57.7	74.6

Category of firm	2009 Percent that use a credit card, by type of card			2010 Percent that use a credit card, by type of card			2011 Percent that use a credit card, by type of card		
	Personal credit card for business purposes	Business credit card	Personal or business credit card	Personal credit card for business purposes	Business credit card	Personal or business credit card	Personal credit card for business purposes	Business credit card	Personal or business credit card
Nonprofessional services	n.r.	n.r.	n.r.	35.6	43.9	67.5	49.0	51.3	76.7
Professional services	n.r.	n.r.	n.r.	43.0	63.3	84.3	42.5	58.2	78.6
Other	n.r.	n.r.	n.r.	45.4	55.2	74.3	41.8	49.7	71.8

Note: Data are representative of small employer firms with 1 to 250 employees in addition to the owner(s) in the year of the survey.

n.a. Not available.

n.r. Not reliable. Due to a skip-pattern problem in the administration of the 2009 questionnaire, detailed statistics on the use of credit cards by firm category are not reliable.

Source: National Federation of Independent Business, annual finance surveys of 2009, 2010, and 2011.

The use of either a personal or business credit card generally increased with the age of the firm. However, unlike with firm size, the distribution between personal and business card use does not show a clear pattern of tradeoffs. At every age, personal card usage is less common than business card usage; however, the usage rate is not highest among the youngest firms.

Credit card usage also varies a great deal by industry. Credit card usage is highest among manufacturing firms, with more than 85 percent of such firms using some type of credit card. In addition, business cards are far more prevalent than personal cards. In 2010, close to 85 percent of finance and real estate businesses and professional services businesses used a personal or business card. Both of these industries saw a decline in the share of firms using cards in 2011. Conversely, the share of construction and mining firms that reported using credit cards grew between 2010 and 2011, from 78.2 percent to 87.5 percent. This increase reflects growth in the share of firms with both personal and business credit cards.

Table 6. Use of trade credit, 2010–11

Percent		
Category of firm	**2010**	**2011**
All firms	57.8	47.1
Number of employees		
0–1	41.6	32.6
2–4	57.2	46.1
5–9	64.0	55.6
10–19	71.2	53.2
20–49	72.2	60.9
50–250	67.2	57.8
Age groups (years)		
Less than 4	42.8	43.8
4–6	54.9	40.0
7–9	54.5	52.6
10–14	59.6	44.0
15–19	60.1	55.6
20–29	57.1	52.6
30 or more	63.0	53.9
Industry		
Construction and mining	83.7	54.2
Manufacturing	55.9	70.9
Wholesale/retail trade	64.5	67.1
Finance/real estate	40.4	31.9
Nonprofessional services	55.3	45.2
Professional services	47.1	38.0
Other	58.4	39.6

Note: Data are representative of small employer firms with 1 to 250 employees in addition to the owner(s) in the year of the survey. Questions on use of trade credit were not asked in the 2009 survey.

Source: National Federation of Independent Business, annual finance surveys of 2010 and 2011.

Trade Credit

Trade credit arises when a business purchases goods or services for which payment is deferred. Like credit cards, firms can use trade credit either as a form of credit or as a convenient alternative to paying cash each time a purchase is made. In 2010, 57.8 percent of small businesses used trade credit, about the same proportion that used credit lines or business loans but much smaller than the proportion that used credit cards (table 6).[28] In 2011, this fraction had fallen to 47.1 percent.

Trade credit is generally extended for an intermediate period (30 to 60 days), at which point payment is due. When payment is not made by the due date, financing charges are applied, and trade credit becomes an alternative method of financing business expenses. Trade credit can be a very costly form of credit for firms that do not make timely payment.

As shown in table 6, trade credit was used more extensively by larger firms (around 70 percent of small businesses with 10 or more employees used trade credit in 2010, compared with 41.6 percent of the smallest firms) and more well-established firms (around 60 percent of small businesses that had been in business 10 or more years used trade credit in 2010, compared with 42.8 percent of the youngest firms). For nearly every size and age category, trade credit was used less in 2011 than it had been in 2010.

Substantial variation in trade credit usage is apparent by industry, with construction and mining firms the most likely to have used trade credit in 2010 but far less likely to have done so in 2011 (83.7 percent in 2010 versus 54.2 percent in 2011). Other industries experienced declines in trade credit usage, although the decreases were not as dramatic. The only industries in which trade credit was more commonly used in 2011 than it had been in 2010 were manufacturing (55.9 percent in 2010 versus 70.9 percent in 2011) and wholesale and retail trade (64.5 percent in 2010 versus 67.1 percent in 2011).

Summary of Credit Use

The use of credit products exhibited several clear patterns. Among small businesses, larger firms were more likely than smaller firms to use each of the traditional credit types. Declines in usage between 2009 and 2011 were also strongest for the smallest firms. However, whether this pattern reflects a greater need for credit at larger firms or whether lenders are simply more willing to extend credit to larger firms is unclear.

The relationship between firm age and credit use is similar to the relationship between size and use, but not as linear. Again, the declines in usage between 2009 and 2011 are most apparent for the youngest firms. Several factors may explain the similarities and differences in the relationships between size and credit use and between firm age and credit use. The similarities are likely due to a correlation between firm size and age most new firms are also quite small. The differences are likely related to the greater informational opacity of younger firms and the different credit needs of firms over their life cycle. The opacity might make evaluating creditworthiness more difficult for lenders, which could reduce the supply of some types of credit available to young firms, while well-established firms may have less need for credit.

Credit Application Experience

In some cases, small businesses may have wanted to use more credit than was reflected in the survey, but were unable to obtain it. The analysis in this section looks at the experience of firms that sought to obtain credit but had their applications denied.

As shown in table 7, one-half of the firms applied for some type of credit in 2009.[29] Just over one-half of these applicants were successful in obtaining all or most of the credit for which they applied. Application rates in 2010 were similar to those in 2009, with nearly two-thirds of firms obtaining all or most of the credit for which they applied. In 2011, the portion of firms applying for credit increased. However, success rates were similar to those observed in 2009, with 46.9 percent of applicants receiving only some or none of the credit for which they applied.

In each year, the larger the firm, the more likely it was to apply for credit. With the exception of the smallest firms, denial rates declined with the number of employees; larger firms' applications were more likely to have been approved.[30] While this is true in each year, both application and denial rates were higher in 2011 than they were in 2009 and 2010.

Application rates and denial rates by firm age do not exhibit a clear pattern. The youngest firms applied more frequently than firms in any other age group in each year except 2011, when they had the same application rate as the oldest firms. The denial rate is generally greatest for firms four to six years old. Between 2009 and 2011, application rates increased for most age groups.

In addition to self-reported application experiences, the NFIB obtained PAYDEX credit scores for surveyed businesses from Dun & Bradstreet. The

PAY-DEX score is a measure of the timeliness with which a business pays its bills; it ranges from 1 to 100, with higher scores indicating more timely payment performance. Some of the apparent differences in application and denial rates can be explained by closer examination of the PAYDEX scores (table 8). The most striking difference is the overall decline in scores between 2010 and 2011. In 2009 and 2010, the average PAYDEX score was 63; in 2011, the average score was less than 45.[31] The PAYDEX scores do provide some support for the notion that younger and smaller firms present more of a risky proposition for potential lenders. Scores generally increase with the age and size of the firm. Thus, the evidence regarding loan application experiences of small businesses and the finding that smaller and younger firms have their loan applications approved less frequently are consistent with the conventional wisdom that these firms are riskier, have shorter credit histories or less collateral to pledge as security, and are more information-ally opaque.

Unfortunately, one cannot tell from the survey data whether the firms that had credit applications denied were able to obtain financing from other sources. Even so, unless all denied credit applications were approved elsewhere, the data on the application experience of firms indicate that the demand for credit by some small businesses may have been higher than suggested by the credit-utilization data. Because smaller and younger firms have their applications denied more frequently than their larger and older peers, the difference between credit demand and ultimate use should be greater at smaller firms.

Besides the firms that were denied credit, some firms that may have wanted additional credit may not have applied because they expected that their applications would be denied. The NFIB surveys asked respondents whether they had forgone applying for needed credit because of the expectation of denial.[32] The data indicate that there may have been a large number of "discouraged borrowers" over this period; in 2009, more than one-third of the sample reported having forgone applying for credit (table 7). While this fraction has declined a bit over time, slightly less than one-third of firms reported having done so in 2011, a share that seems elevated.[33] It is important to keep in mind that not all credit applications *should* be approved. It is clear from table 8 that the firms that did not apply for credit because they felt the application would be turned down were less creditworthy, with credit scores 7 to 15 points below those of the average firm.

Table 7. Overall credit application experience, 2009–11

Category of firm	2009			2010			2011		
	Applied for any credit	Got none or some of credit applied for	Didn't apply for fear of rejection	Applied for any credit	Got none or some of credit applied for	Didn't apply for fear of rejection	Applied for any credit	Got none or some of credit applied for	Didn't apply for fear of rejection
All firms	**50.4**	**49.4**	**36.7**	**48.2**	**36.8**	**25.0**	**56.5**	**46.9**	**29.4**
Number of employees									
0–1	43.2	45.2	31.3	36.4	32.0	28.6	48.3	26.2	19.5
2–4	50.0	60.9	48.5	45.7	40.7	23.3	53.3	61.4	36.4
5–9	47.9	40.6	23.5	49.6	40.3	29.9	61.3	49.4	35.6
10–19	59.7	47.8	39.2	58.8	33.6	24.9	63.4	38.7	17.7
20–49	61.3	36.2	26.0	65.7	35.3	23.4	67.2	42.7	25.9
50–250	63.5	27.3	17.6	78.8	23.5	11.2	77.2	32.0	20.3
Age groups (years)									
Less than 4	58.7	69.1	52.8	53.1	28.9	20.8	61.3	50.1	26.5
4–6	47.3	65.0	49.9	49.6	65.4	47.2	49.6	59.1	28.8
7–9	56.5	43.5	38.2	44.9	35.5	34.3	59.4	50.9	41.6
10–14	49.9	38.5	32.3	47.2	38.8	28.7	49.5	47.7	38.7
15–19	45.9	53.3	29.6	45.1	39.9	22.8	58.7	22.4	20.7
20–29	52.1	38.3	27.8	46.1	32.4	22.2	52.9	46.3	28.1
30 or more	44.1	50.1	37.5	51.5	26.9	14.9	61.4	30.8	24.3
Industry									
Construction and mining	57.1	46.1	32.7	56.8	26.9	21.1	63.4	43.7	21.9
Manufacturing	63.5	51.1	45.7	49.6	21.6	14.2	59.3	42.8	27.5
Wholesale/retail trade	46.9	40.4	27.4	42.4	36.4	23.3	56.9	46.0	29.6
Finance/real estate	58.6	61.6	47.3	52.3	49.4	18.8	49.7	53.8	32.9
Nonprofessional services	41.9	50.3	36.7	43.1	50.1	29.4	56.5	44.3	25.2
Professional services	50.7	50.3	36.1	46.7	41.8	35.6	52.0	49.9	33.8
Other	48.8	56.9	41.3	58.4	18.8	19.7	60.8	47.4	34.9

Note: Data are representative of small employer firms with 1 to 250 employees in addition to the owner(s) in the year of the survey.

Source: National Federation of Independent Business, annual finance surveys of 2009, 2010, and 2011.

Table 8. Average PAYDEX score, 2009–11

Percent			
Category of firm	**2009**	**2010**	**2011**
All firms	**63.1**	**63.0**	**44.7**
Didn't apply because felt application would be denied	54.4	47.8	38.0
Number of employees			
0–1	56.3	64.1	42.5
2–4	60.3	58.8	42.5
5–9	69.3	64.9	47.3
10–19	70.8	67.5	47.2
20–49	69.1	65.7	49.4
50–250	71.6	75.0	52.2
Age groups (years)			
Less than 4	52.0	52.7	38.4
4–6	54.9	48.3	40.9
7–9	51.7	53.3	47.4
10–14	70.3	54.8	44.5
15–19	67.2	68.1	52.3
20–29	64.8	69.0	49.1
30 or more	68.1	74.8	54.5
Industry			
Construction and mining	62.6	63.8	38.8
Manufacturing	63.5	59.0	51.3
Wholesale/retail trade	66.3	64.8	48.2
Finance/real estate	67.5	68.1	46.7
Nonprofessional services	56.5	57.2	41.7
Professional services	66.2	63.9	44.7
Other	58.3	65.0	47.5

Note: Data are representative of small employer firms with 1 to 250 employees in addition to the owner(s) in the year of the survey. The PAYDEX score is a measure of the timeliness with which a business pays its bills; it ranges from 1 to 100, with higher scores indicating more timely payment performance.

Source: National Federation of Independent Business, annual finance surveys of 2009, 2010, and 2011.

Overall, credit use by small business has declined in recent years. This decline is likely a combination of several supply and demand factors. First, as noted earlier in this chapter, the demand for credit started to decrease around 2006 and plummeted in 2008, recovering only partially at present. Second, also as discussed previously, credit generally became less available as banks tightened their standards. Finally, small businesses' financial health and their ability to pay their bills in a timely fashion have generally deteriorated over this time, making it more difficult to borrow even if the firms desired to do so.

PROVIDERS OF CREDIT TO SMALL BUSINESSES

This section examines providers of small business credit, which include commercial banks, savings institutions, credit unions, finance companies, nonfinancial firms, and individuals such as family members or friends.[34] Because commercial banks traditionally have been the leading source of credit to small businesses, the analysis focuses primarily on their activities. This section explores the relationship between bank size and small business lending and discusses the concentration of small business lending by commercial banks. The section also presents a more modest analysis of small business lending by savings institutions, credit unions, and some nondepository institutions, which account for substantially less small business credit than commercial banks. Together, these issues can provide insight into the availability of credit to small businesses.

Overview

Past survey data highlighted the importance of depository institutions to small business credit availability. According to the 2003 Survey of Small Business Finances (SSBF), more than 60 percent of small businesses had outstanding credit lines, loans, or leases.[35] Commercial banks provided credit lines, loans, or leases to 41.1 percent of small firms, a proportion that corresponds to about 68 percent of the small firms that obtained a traditional form of credit from any source. In addition, 5.5 percent of small businesses obtained traditional credit from a savings bank or a savings and loan association, and 3.9 percent obtained it from a credit union. In total, depository institutions supplied credit to more than three-fourths of the businesses that reported having outstanding credit.

Nondepositories, which include both financial and nonfinancial firms, provided credit to about one-third of small businesses in 2003. The key sources of credit among nondepository financial firms were finance companies (22.2 percent of firms) and leasing companies (4.3 percent). Family and individuals (6.5 percent) were the most important nonfinancial source of credit.

Commercial banks were, by a wide margin, the most common source of virtually every credit product included in the survey. They supplied more small businesses with lines of credit, mortgage loans, and equipment loans than any other type of provider. They were also the second most common supplier of motor vehicle loans and "other" loans.[36] Finance companies were the most important sources of motor vehicle loans and leases, whereas family and friends were the most important sources of other loans.

More-current data suggest the continued importance of commercial banks to small businesses in recent years. According to the 2010 Survey of Consumer Finances (SCF), 78.4 percent of households that owned small businesses indicated that the primary institution for their business was a commercial bank.[37] Similarly in 2011, over 85 percent of small businesses in the most recent NFIB finance survey reported that their primary financial institution was a commercial bank.[38] According to both surveys, non-depository institutions are rarely the firm's primary institution.

Beyond survey data, an important source of information on the small business lending activities of commercial banks and savings institutions is the small business loan data collected by the Federal Reserve and other regulatory agencies on the Reports of Condition and Income (Call Reports) and Thrift Financial Reports (TFRs).[39] These data, which have been collected annually since June 1993 and quarterly since March 2010, include information on outstanding small C&I loans and loans secured by nonfarm, nonresidential properties.[40] The number of loans and amount outstanding are collected for loans with original amounts of $100,000 or less, more than $100,000 but less than $250,000, and more than $250,000 but less than $1 million.[41]

These data are used to estimate the amount of credit extended to small firms. Because firm characteristics are not reported on Call Reports or TFRs, loan size is often used as a proxy for the size of the firm receiving credit. However, this approach to measuring small business lending introduces two sources of inaccuracy in the measurement of the number and dollar amount of loans to small businesses. First, the data likely include loans equal to or less than $1 million extended to large firms, and second, the data exclude loans of more than $1 million made to small firms.[42] According to the 2003 SSBF, only about 3.5 percent of credit-line extensions to small businesses were associated with commitments greater than $1 million. However, these relatively few loan extensions accounted for roughly two-thirds of the dollar value of credit-line commitments to small businesses. Although a large share of the total dollar value of small business loans may be excluded from what is considered a small business loan on the Call Report and TFR data, these loans are not typical of the credit obtained by the majority of small firms.[43] According to data from Community Reinvestment Act (CRA) reporters, a little more than one-third of the loan dollar volume of loans with initial values of less than $1 million dollars is directed to firms with revenues of less than $1 million. This volume is likely to be an understatement since many reporters do not collect or submit information on the revenues of the firms they lend to. This result does indicate, however, that a significant portion of loans included in the less than $1 million category are made to larger businesses. It is not possible to tell which inaccuracy is likely to be larger.

Lending by Depository Institutions

Commercial Banks

Commercial banks are important providers of credit to small firms.[44] Lending to small businesses involves unique challenges that banks are particularly well suited to meet. Of particular significance, information on the financial condition, performance, and prospects of small firms is not readily available, so lending is often based heavily on information gathered through established relationships, which banks and their staff frequently have with small firms and their owners. Commercial banks continue to maintain local branch networks, which further aid them in gathering such information. Commercial banks have continued providing credit to small businesses through business credit cards, which rely on business or consumer credit ratings rather than established relationships.

Bank Size

The relationship between bank size and the extent to which banks engage in small business lending may have implications for the availability of credit to small firms. Substantial consolidation in the banking industry over the past 25 years has dramatically reduced the number of banks, increasing the importance of large banks and the concentration of industry assets.[45] For example, more than 2,800 bank mergers involving acquired assets in excess of $4.3 trillion were completed between 1999 and 2011.[46] Even though more than 1,500 new banks were granted charters over this period, the total number of bank organizations fell by more than 15 percent to 5,670 (table 9).

One merger-related structural development that has raised concerns about the availability of credit to small businesses stems from the fact that large banks tend to be proportionately less committed than smaller banks to small business lending. As seen in table 10, the average banking organization with $1 billion or less in total assets held over 15 percent of its portfolio as small business loans in June 2011.[47] In contrast, organizations with assets between $1 billion and $10 billion held almost 12 percent of their assets as small business loans, and the largest organizations—those with assets greater than $10 billion held only about 5 percent of their assets as such loans. Small business loans play a larger role in the portfolios of small banks than they do in the portfolios of large institutions.

The pattern for holdings of microloans, which are defined as business loans of $100,000 or less, is even clearer, with smaller banks maintaining an even larger share of their asset portfolios in such loans. The smallest banks tend to be proportionately more invested in the smallest business loans for two primary reasons. First, many small banks provide banking services to a particular local area. As a result, these banks are likely to accumulate knowledge of their local markets, which is often important in making risky, relationship-dependent small business loans. Difficulties in evaluating and monitoring loans likely become more severe as firms, and therefore loans, decrease in size. Second, bank regulations limit the amount that a bank can lend to a single borrower to 25 percent of the bank's capital; by definition, small banks are limited by their assets in their ability to make very large loans. Small banks can also maintain a more diversified portfolio by making many smaller loans, rather than fewer larger loans.

Table 9. Structural measures and the size of the U.S. commerical banking industry, 1999–2011 (selected years)

Year (as of June 30)	Number		Total assets held by insured U.S. commercial banks (billions of dollars)	Share of domestic commercial banking assets held by the largest organizations (percent)			
	Commercial banking organizations[1]	Insured U.S. commercial banks		Top 10	Top 25	Top 50	Top 100
1999	6,720	8,499	4,576	40.1	55.9	68.6	76.1
2003	6,390	7,675	6,282	45.8	61.4	71.8	78.1
2007	6,134	7,203	8,444	51.4	66.4	74.4	79.6
2011	5,670	6,302	10,285	56.0	70.5	77.8	82.4

Note: Includes insured U.S. domestically chartered banks excluding credit card institutions.

[1] Commerical banking organizations include bank holding companies and independent banks.

Source: Call Reports (June 30), various years; National Information Center database.

Table 10. Average small business loan and microloan holdings as a share of assets for U.S. commercial banking organizations of different sizes, 2011

Percent except as noted			
Asset class	**Number of banking organizations[1]**	**Small business loans to assets**	**Microloan holdings to assets**
All organizations	**5,670**	**16.0**	**3.6**
$250 million or less	3,785	16.9	4.5
$250 million to $1 billion[2]	1,418	15.1	2.1
$1 billion to $10 billion[2]	399	11.5	1.4
More than $10 billion	68	5.5	.9

Note: Small business loans are business loans of $1 million or less; microloans, a subset of small business loans, are for $100,000 or less. U.S. commerical banking organizations are insured U.S. domestically chartered banks excluding credit card institutions and U.S. branches and agencies of foreign banks.

[1] Banking organizations include bank holding companies and independent banks.

[2] Banks with assets of $1 billion are included in the $250 million to $1 billion size class, and banks with assets of $10 billion are included in the $1 billion to $10 billion size class.

Source: Call Reports (June 30); National Information Center database.

Even though small business lending represents a smaller share of banking activity by the largest banking organizations, these banks are still significant providers of small business loans. Banking organizations with assets greater than $10 billion accounted for 1.2 percent of all commercial banking organizations in June 2011 but held 80.0 percent of the banking assets in the industry (table 11). These large organizations held a much smaller, but nonetheless substantial, share of small business loans, as 47.9 percent of small business loan dollars and 63.0 percent of microloan dollars were held by banking organizations with more than $10 billion in assets. They also account for a substantial portion of the number of loans granted, extending almost 87 percent of all microloans and almost 44 percent of business loans greater than $100,000 but less than $1 million. The only microloan or small business loan category to increase between 2007 and 2011 was that for microloans by banking organizations with more than $10 billion in assets. Small business loans for all other banks decreased (table 12).

Table 11. Share of small business loan and microloan holdings of U.S. commercial banking organizations, by asset class, 2007 and 2011

Asset class	Share of banking organizations[1]	Share of industry assets	Share of holdings		Share of loans extended	
			Small business loans	Microloans	Small business loans	Microloans
2007						
$250 million or less	72.1	5.1	14.4	18.2	12.9	7.7
$250 million to $1 billion[2]	21.0	7.2	17.8	14.1	8.2	6.8
$1 billion to $10 billion[2]	5.8	11.1	19.4	13.2	9.5	7.9
More than $10 billion	1.1	76.6	48.4	54.5	69.4	77.7
2011						
$250 million or less	66.8	4.0	13.7	13.9	5.4	4.3
$250 million to $1 billion[2]	25.0	6.4	18.3	11.9	5.7	3.9
$1 billion to $10 billion[2]	7.0	9.6	20.1	11.2	6.9	4.8
More than $10 billion	1.2	80.0	47.9	63.0	82.0	86.9

Note: Small business loans are business loans of $1 million or less; microloans, a subset of small business loans, are for $100,000 or less. U.S. commerical banking organizations are insured U.S. domestically chartered banks excluding credit card institutions and U.S. branches and agencies of foreign banks.

[1] Banking organizations include bank holding companies and independent banks.

[2] Banks with assets of $1 billion are included in the $250 million to $1 billion size class, and banks with assets of $10 billion are included in the $1 billion to $10 billion size class.

Source: Call Reports (June 30); National Information Center database.

Despite their declining numbers and a fall in their share of industry assets, small banks continue to account for a sizable share of small business loans. In 2011, banks with assets of $250 million or less accounted for 66.8 percent of all banking organizations but only 4.0 percent of all banking assets (table 11).

However, they held 13.7 percent of all small business loans and 13.9 percent of microloans.

The share of small business loan dollars held by organizations with assets greater than $10 billion fell slightly between 2007 and 2011, but the share of business microloan dollars for these institutions increased from 54.5 percent to 63.0 percent. In 1997, the share of microloans held by banking organizations with assets greater than $10 billion was only 30.6 percent. The pattern for the number of loans extended is similar to that for total dollar values. The growth in the share of business microloans since 1997 reflects the increasing importance of large banking organizations in providing the smallest loans. Increased use of sophisticated technological and analytical tools, particularly credit-scoring techniques, may have contributed to the rise in the share of microloans held and originated by large banking organizations. The largest banks may also have expertise in credit card programs and may have leveraged this experience to provide business credit cards that typically have low balances (Brevoort and Hannan, 2006).

The lending shares of the smallest banks those with assets of $250 million or less decreased between 2007 and 2011. Some of this decrease was due to the reduction in the share of banking organizations and bank assets that, because of bank consolidation, occurred for this class of institutions. The decrease in the share of small loan holdings at the smallest banks was comparable with the increases experienced by banks with assets between $250 million and $1 billion and banks with assets of $1 billion to $10 billion. Conversely, increases in the shares of microloan holdings and the share of small loans and microloans extended were observed only for the largest banks.

Numerous research studies directly analyze the relationship between consolidation activity and the availability of credit to small firms.[48] Although mergers and acquisitions sever existing bank firm relationships and may introduce some short-term uncertainty (Berger and Udell, 1998), the results of the research generally suggest that overall they have not materially reduced credit availability.

One issue that has been addressed is the effect of mergers on the small business lending activities of the banks directly involved in those mergers. The results of these studies generally indicate that deals involving at least one large bank tend to reduce small business loans as a share of assets, whereas deals between two small banks tend to increase small business loans as a share of assets (for example, Critchfield and others, 2004; Avery and Samolyk, 2000, 2004; Samolyk and Richardson, 2003; Peek and Rosengren, 1998; and Strahan and Weston, 1998).

Table 12. Growth of small business loan and microloan holdings of U.S. commercial banking organizations, by asset class, 2003–07 and 2007–11

Percent						
	2003–07			2007-11		
Asset class	Microloan growth	Small loans growth	Total loan growth	Microloan growth	Small loans growth	Total loan growth
All organizations	**1.8**	**5.9**	**10.5**	**-2.7**	**-2.8**	**2.1**
$250 million or less	-6.1	-2.0	.4	-7.9	-3.9	-2.8
$250 million to $1 billion[1]	-1.6	5.0	9.4	-6.2	-2.1	-.6
$1 billion to $10 billion[1]	3.5	9.0	12.5	-6.0	-1.9	-1.0
More than $10 billion	7.1	8.4	11.3	.8	-3.0	3.3

Note: Small business loans are business loans of $1 million or less; microloans, a subset of small business loans, are for $100,000 or less. U.S. commercial banking organizations are insured U.S. domestically chartered banks excluding credit card institutions and U.S. branches and agencies of foreign banks. No adjustments are made for banks that change asset classes during the period.

[1] Banks with assets of $1 billion are included in the $250 million to $1 billion size class, and banks with assets of $10 billion are included in the $1 billion to $10 billion size class.

Source: Call Reports (June 30); National Information Center database.

Both results are relevant to assessing the influence of consolidation on the availability of small business credit from banks and savings institutions. On the one hand, about 89 percent of the bank assets acquired between 1999 and 2011 belonged to banks with at least $1 billion in total assets. Therefore, a large majority of the banking assets that have changed hands have been purchased in deals in which a decline in small business loans, as a share of assets, typically takes place at the consolidated bank.

On the other hand, even though relatively few assets have been purchased in mergers of small institutions, deals involving target banks with total assets of $250 million or less accounted for nearly two-thirds of all transactions completed between 1999 and 2011. About 19 percent of these deals involved an acquirer that had assets of $250 million or less, and roughly 26 percent involved an acquirer with assets between $250 million and $1 billion. Even though relatively few assets have been acquired in a deal typically associated with an increase in small business lending ratios, nearly three-fifths of all deals have occurred with small- or medium-sized acquirers. Therefore, after merger activity, many banks have had an overall increase in the share of their asset portfolios dedicated to small business lending.

Another issue that has been studied is the "external" effect of mergers that is, what happens to small business lending at banks that compete directly with recently merged institutions. Evidence suggests that banks competing with recent merger participants tend to increase their lending (Berger and others, 1998; and Berger, Goldberg, and White, 2001). Two other empirical findings suggest that a growing amount of credit may be supplied by banks that compete with recently merged banks. First, consolidation increases the likelihood of new entry into a market (Adams and Amel, 2007; Berger and others, 2004; Seelig and Critchfield, 2003; and Keeton, 2000). Second, younger banks tend to make more small business loans than similar, but more mature, institutions (DeYoung, Goldberg, and White, 1999). These two empirical findings suggest that a common response to merger activity is greater entry of new banks, which tend to be active lenders to small businesses.

From the perspective of small firms, the effect of banking consolidation on credit availability may not be especially substantial given that the size of the banks operating in a market appears not to affect the availability of credit. Small businesses in areas with few small banks are no more credit constrained than small businesses in areas with many small banks (Jayaratne and Wolken, 1999). In addition, the likelihood that a small business will borrow from a bank of a given size is roughly proportional to the local presence of banks of that size, although some evidence shows that small banks are more likely to make very small loans (Berger, Rosen, and Udell, 2001). In sum, the potential gap in credit availability to small businesses due to bank consolidation by the largest banks is usually attenuated by competition from small and medium-sized banks, by the entry of new banks, and by the substitution of credit extended by nonbank financial institutions for that extended by commercial banks (Ou, 2005; and Craig and Hardee, 2007).[49]

Industry Structure

As large banks have acquired other institutions, especially other large ones, the number of banks has declined, and the size of the largest banks has increased. These developments may enable the most active lenders to account for a growing share of all small business lending. In this section, the distribution of small business loan holdings at the industry level is analyzed to assess the importance of the leading small business lenders in the overall provision of small business credit.

Data on industry structure in table 13 indicate that the leading small business loan holders account for a small share of loans relative to the share of total assets they hold. For instance, in 2011, the 10 leading holders of small business loans held 29.9 percent of all such loans and 51.2 percent of all banking assets. Similar differences between the share of small business loans and the share of total assets are observed among the 25, 50, and 100 leading small business loan holders. This pattern has two implications for the availability of credit to small businesses. First, because the share of small business lending activity attributable to the most active lenders is smaller than their share of total assets, the relatively less active small lenders remain a key source of credit for small firms. Second, although the share of small business lending attributable to the leading banks has increased, particularly with respect to microloans, an industry in which the dominant providers of credit to small businesses are a relatively few large banking organizations does not appear to be developing.

Table 13. Share of assets and small business loan and microloan holdings of leading U.S. commercial banking organizations, 2007 and 2011

Percent				
Leading banking organizations[1]	Share held by leading holders of small business loans		Share held by leading holders of microloans	
	Small business loans	Assets	Microloans	Assets
2007				
Top 10	28.2	51.0	39.7	45.6
Top 25	39.7	63.8	48.9	62.7
Top 50	47.5	71.6	55.0	70.6
Top 100	54.7	75.8	59.8	75.4
2011				
Top 10	29.9	51.2	50.3	50.1
Top 25	40.5	64.9	58.8	64.9
Top 50	47.1	72.0	63.2	71.9
Top 100	54.0	76.0	67.3	75.2

Note: Small business loans are business loans of $1 million or less; microloans, a subset of small business loans, are for $100,000 or less. U.S. commercial banking organizations are insured U.S. domestically chartered banks excluding credit card institutions and U.S. branches and agencies of foreign banks. For each category of loan activity, leading banking organizations account for the greatest share of that category.

[1] Banking organizations include bank holding companies and independent banks.

Source: Call Reports (June 30); National Information Center database.

These data also show that the shares of small business loans held by the most active small business lenders have remained relatively constant since 2007, as have the shares of banking assets for these firms. The 100 most active small business bank lenders accounted for just over one-half of the outstanding small business loans and three-quarters of total assets in both 2007 and 2011. Microloan lending became slightly more concentrated with the top 100 most active small business bank lenders, accounting for over 67 percent of microloans in 2011, up from slightly less than 60 percent in 2007.

Although large banking organizations are proportionately less active in small business lending than smaller banks, the leading small business lenders nonetheless typically include the largest banking organizations. For example, in 2007 and 2011, the top 10 holders of small business loans were among the 15 largest banking organizations in the industry.

Local Lending Patterns

The relevant market for many small business loans remains local. The structure of the local banking market is particularly important because changes in concentration could affect the level of competition for small business lending, which, in turn, could influence the cost of borrowing and the quantity of credit demanded. To address some key issues associated with the availability of credit to small businesses, one must shift the analysis from lending at the industry level. Instead, analysis of bank structure within smaller geographic areas is likely to capture more accurately the relevant market conditions that small firms face when seeking credit, and that influence competition in the market for small business loans.

Previous data from the SSBFs indicate that a small business tends to obtain loans, leases, and lines of credit from a nearby provider.[50] In 2003, the median distance between a small business and its lender was 11 miles, and in 66.0 percent of all business-lending relationships, the lender was located within 30 miles of the firm's headquarters. For depository institutions and banks, the major suppliers of small business credit, lenders were located even closer the median distance was 4 miles, and 83.0 percent of lenders were located within 30 miles of the firm's headquarters. More-current data from the 2010 SCF reinforce this pattern. Among households that report owning businesses with fewer than 500 employees, the median distance to their firm's primary financial institution was 3 miles.

This proximity offers small firms convenient access to their lenders. Also, banks have traditionally preferred to extend loans to small businesses near their branches. The importance of relationships in small business lending suggests that credit providers concentrate their lending activities in geographic areas with which they are familiar (Berger and Udell, 1998; Brevoort and Hannan, 2006; Critchfield and others, 2004; and Scott, Dunkelberg, and Dennis, 2003).

Local Market Concentration

Conventional economic theory predicts, and empirical evidence suggests, that highly concentrated markets exhibit less competition, which results in higher prices and the provision of less credit. Some theories, however, predict that a less competitive lending environment may increase credit availability to at least some firms by allowing local banks more flexibility in structuring loan programs over time to the extent that it promotes longer-term relationships (for example, Petersen and Rajan, 1995). Long-term relationships, which facilitate loans to many small businesses, may be more difficult to maintain in highly competitive markets because businesses that are earning good profits will likely seek out the lender offering the most favorable, low-cost loan terms. A bank in a less competitive market might offer a below-market interest rate on a loan to help a new business or an ongoing firm experiencing hard times, with the expectation that the bank will receive above-market returns on loans when the business is operating successfully. To date, tests of these theories have produced mixed results.[51]

Data from the annual Summary of Deposits, which reports the location and deposit level of every commercial bank, savings bank, and savings and loan branch as of June 30, are used to examine bank market structure and competition in local areas.[52] The primary measure used by antitrust authorities to assess market concentration is the deposit-based Herfindahl-Hirschman Index (HHI), which is computed as the sum of the squared market shares (that is, the shares of total deposits) of each firm in a market. These measures are shown in table 14, along with information on the number of banks and banking offices.[53] The data show that, in 2011, about 27 banks with 208 offices provided banking services in the average metropolitan statistical area (MSA). The average level of the HHI with 50 percent thrift inclusion was 1664.[54] In the average micropolitan area, 9 banks with 21 branches provided services. The average HHI with 50 percent thrift inclusion was 2285. Rural areas are much more highly concentrated with respect to their deposits and, on average, have fewer banks and banking offices. In 2011, the average rural market had about 4.4 banks with 7 offices. The average rural market HHI with 50 percent thrift inclusion was 4137.

Table 14. Average structural measures of U.S. commercial banking and thrift organizations, by metropolitan statistical area, micropolitan area, and rural county, 1999–2011

Year	MSA				Micropolitan area				Rural county			
	Number of banks	HHI50	Number of offices	Population per office	Number of banks	HHI50	Number of offices	Population per office	Number of banks	HHI50	Number of offices	Population per office
1999	24.3	1735	171.1	3,439	8.2	2377	19.8	2,767	4.2	4306	7.1	2,160
2000	24.8	1723	173.7	3,479	8.3	2363	20.0	2,802	4.2	4273	7.1	2,188
2001	24.8	1695	174.9	3,496	8.3	2348	20.2	2,784	4.3	4238	7.2	2,150
2002	24.7	1702	175.8	3,514	8.3	2341	20.2	2,787	4.3	4229	7.2	2,145
2003	24.9	1699	179.0	3,503	8.4	2327	20.3	2,785	4.3	4214	7.2	2,140
2004	25.1	1705	184.2	3,471	8.5	2306	20.4	2,776	4.3	4209	7.3	2,136
2005	25.3	1726	189.9	3,429	8.6	2299	20.7	2,748	4.4	4187	7.3	2,135
2006	26.1	1694	196.6	3,372	8.7	2282	20.9	2,733	4.4	4134	7.3	2,122
2007	26.6	1684	202.7	3,325	8.8	2269	21.3	2,703	4.4	4130	7.4	2,109
2008	27.4	1625	209.2	3,277	9.0	2281	21.6	2,681	4.4	4131	7.4	2,094
2009	27.3	1664	210.2	3,291	9.1	2281	21.6	2,683	4.4	4114	7.4	2,087
2010	26.9	1637	207.9	3,379	9.1	2281	21.5	2,738	4.4	4124	7.4	2,146
2011	26.8	1664	207.6	3,415	9.1	2285	21.4	2,773	4.4	4137	7.3	2,157

Note: U.S. commercial banking organizations and thrifts are insured U.S. domestically chartered banks and insured U.S. domestically chartered savings banks and savings and loan associations excluding credit card institutions and U.S. branches and agencies of foreign banks. Definitions of metropolitan statistical areas (MSAs) and micropolitan areas refer to 2004 definitions. HHI50 is the deposit-based Herfindahl-Hirschman Index with 50 percent thrift inclusion. Offices are those with deposits greater than or equal to zero.

Source: Call Reports (June 30); Thrift Financial Reports (June 30); Summary of Deposits; National Information Center database; U.S. Census Bureau area definitions.

Comparing these indexes with those of earlier years, we find that despite the significant amount of consolidation in the banking industry, local banking markets do not appear to have become more concentrated. Generally, in rural, micropolitan, and MSA markets, the number of banks and offices has remained constant or increased somewhat, whereas the HHIs have either remained constant or decreased somewhat. Modest deconcentration, in conjunction with a small increase in the number of banks, suggests that a reduction in competition from commercial banking organizations is not likely to have been a contributing factor in the decline in the availability of credit in recent years.

Overall, small business loans outstanding from commercial banks peaked in 2008 and have declined in each subsequent year (table 1). Despite significant industry consolidation, concentration in local banking markets the geographic units that are most relevant for small business lending did not increase, on average, over the past decade. This fact suggests that the observed decline in small business loans outstanding was not due to reduced competition among commercial banks in the provision of credit to small businesses. Rather, the decrease in small business lending by commercial banks was likely caused by a combination of a reduction in demand for credit on the part of small businesses, a decline in the credit quality of many potential small business borrowers, and a tightening of terms and standards on the part of commercial banks. In addition, some of the decrease was likely due to deterioration in the financial condition of many banks during this period.[55]

Savings Institutions

Savings institutions, defined as savings banks and savings and loan associations, provide much less credit to small businesses than do commercial banks. The primary lines of business for these institutions, often referred to as thrifts, tend to involve providing retail financial services, such as residential mortgage loans, savings accounts, and negotiable order of withdrawal (or NOW) accounts, to households.[56] As of June 30, 2011, there were 1,057 thrifts and 5,670 commercial banking organizations. The value of small business loans held by savings institutions was slightly more than one-tenth of the value held by banks. Savings institutions held $62.9 billion in small business loans and $21.8 billion in microloans, compared with $529.7 billion and $111.2 billion, respectively, held by commercial banks.

Table 15. Structural measures and the size of insured U.S. savings institutions, 1999–2011 (selected years)

Year (as of June 30)	Number	Total assets held by insured U.S. thrifts and savings banks (billions of dollars)	Share of domestic savings assets held by the largest organizations (percent)			
	Insured U.S. thrifts and savings banks		Top 10	Top 25	Top 50	Top 100
1999	1,570	1,115	36.6	51.1	61.9	71.5
2003	1,359	1,423	40.3	54.8	67.3	76.3
2007	1,200	1,833	48.7	64.0	75.3	82.2
2011	1,057	1,219	41.5	57.6	67.7	76.1

Note: Insured U.S. savings institutions include insured U.S. domestically chartered savings banks and savings and loan associations excluding credit card institutions.
Source: Call Reports (June 30); Thrift Financial Reports (June 30); National Information Center database.

These differences between commercial banks and savings institutions reflect both the disparity in overall size between the two groups of institutions and the lower proportion of small business lending conducted by the typical savings institution. In 2011, roughly $11.5 trillion in total assets were held by commercial banks and savings institutions, with the latter holding about 10 percent of the total, or $1.2 trillion (table 15). Overall, in 2011, the average thrift held roughly 9.0 percent of its asset portfolio in small business loans and 1.3 percent in microloans (table 16). In contrast, the average commercial bank held 16.0 percent of its portfolio in small business loans and 3.6 percent in microloans (table 10). These substantial differences in small business lending activity between banks and thrifts clearly indicate that the typical savings institution has been much less active than the typical commercial bank in providing credit to small firms.[57]

Among savings institutions, the most active lenders to small businesses were not necessarily the largest institutions in terms of assets. In 2011, the 10 most active thrifts accounted for 55.0 percent of thrift small business lending (table 17). In 2007, the 10 most active thrifts accounted for a much greater proportion of thrift assets than they did in 2011, falling by over 10 percentage points from 31.6 percent to 20.8 percent. The failure of the largest thrift, Washington Mutual in 2008, contributed to this dramatic change in the asset holdings of the most active thrifts. Prior to its failure, Washington Mutual held 19.0 percent of total thrift assets and accounted for 3.5 percent of total small business loans. Despite its size, the failure of Washington Mutual does not seem to have disproportionately affected the availability of loans to small businesses from thrifts; the decline in outstanding small business loans at thrifts between 2007 and 2011 was similar to the decline at commercial banks.

Thrift microloan lending is highly concentrated. In 2007, the 10 most active lenders accounted for 85.2 percent of thrift microloan outstandings. By 2011, the top 10's share had increased to 88.9 percent. However, unlike commercial banks, the most active microloan lenders are not necessarily the largest institutions. In 2011, while the 10 most active lenders accounted for almost nine-tenths of thrift microloan dollars outstanding, they held less than one-fourth of total thrift assets.

Credit Unions

A credit union is a not-for-profit financial cooperative, owned and controlled by the people who use its services. Credit unions offer many of the same financial services that banks do. Like savings institutions, credit unions have not historically provided a great deal of credit to small businesses. According to the 2003 SSBF, credit unions provided less than 1 percent of aggregate dollars outstanding to small businesses.

Table 16. Average small business loan and microloan holdings as a share of assets for U.S. savings institutions and thrifts of different sizes, 2011

Percent except as noted			
Asset class	**Number of savings institutions**	**Small business loans to assets**	**Microloan holdings to assets**
All organizations	**1,057**	**9.0**	**1.3**
$250 million or less	576	9.7	1.6
$250 million to $1 billion[1]	332	9.3	1.0
$1 billion to $10 billion[1]	128	6.0	.7
More than $10 billion	21	4.5	2.8

Note: Small business loans are business loans of $1 million or less; microloans, a subset of small business loans, are for $100,000 or less. Insured U.S. savings institutions include insured U.S. domestically chartered savings banks and savings and loan associations excluding credit card institutions.

[1] Banks with assets of $1 billion are included in the $250 million to $1 billion size class, and banks with assets of $10 billion are included in the $1 billion to $10 billion size class.

Source: Call Reports (June 30); Thrift Financial Reports (June 30); National Information Center database.

Table 17. Share of assets and small business loan and microloan holdings of leading U.S. savings institutions and thrifts, 2007 and 2011

Percent				
Leading savings institutions	Share held by leading holders of small business loans		Share held by leading holders of microloans	
	Small business loans	Assets	Microloans	Assets
2007				
Top 10	52.1	31.6	85.2	31.6
Top 25	60.9	38.2	88.2	33.5
Top 50	69.3	43.1	91.0	37.7
Top 100	79.1	48.8	94.0	42.9
2011				
Top 10	55.0	20.8	88.9	22.4
Top 25	63.9	30.1	91.6	26.5
Top 50	71.9	38.5	93.7	30.3
Top 100	81.1	45.5	95.9	35.0

Note: Holdings of thrift institutions are tabulated at the entity level. Small business loans are business loans of $1 million or less; microloans, a subset of small business loans, are for $100,000 or less. Insured U.S. savings institutions include insured U.S. domestically chartered savings banks and savings and loan associations excluding credit card institutions. For each category of loan activity, leading banking organizations account for the greatest share of that category.

Source: Call Reports (June 30); Thrift Financial Reports (June 30); National Information Center database.

However, credit unions have become a more important source of small business loans in recent years. In the 2009 NFIB survey, fewer than 4 percent of firms reported using a credit union as their primary financial institution. By 2010, this figure had increased to just less than 5 percent, and it was near 7 percent by 2011. Similarly, 7.1 percent of households that owned small businesses in the 2010 SCF reported using a credit union as the firm's primary financial institution.

Although outstanding small loans to businesses by credit unions remain a small fraction of those by commercial banks, they have increased steadily throughout the recession and post-recession period, while commercial banks' small loans to businesses have shrunk (table 18). Between 2007 and 2011, credit union outstanding loans to business members *increased* by 54.5 percent, while outstanding small loans to businesses by commercial banks *decreased* by 11.1 percent.[58]

Table 18. Business loan holdings of federally insured U.S. credit unions, 2007–11

Year	Total business loans (billions of dollars)	Total business loans less unfunded commitments (billions of dollars)	Number of business loans
2007	24.6	22.6	130,741
2008	29.7	27.8	140,113
2009	33.7	32.0	157,411
2010	36.2	34.6	160,478
2011	37.9	36.3	170,692

Note: Business loans include construction and land development loans and agricultural loans, unlike in the previous tables.

Source: Quarterly credit union reporting forms (June 30).

Since 1998, credit union lending to member businesses has been subject to a cap of 12.25 percent of total assets. Before the passage of the Credit Union Membership Access Act of 1998, there was no limit to the amount that credit unions could lend to member businesses. Bills that would increase the cap to 25 percent of assets are currently pending in both the House and the Senate.[59] As of June 2011, 3.6 percent of credit unions had outstanding loans to business members totaling at least 10 percent of their assets. Among the largest credit unions those with assets of more than $1 billion—13.9 percent had outstanding loans to business members that were at least 10 percent of their assets. Thus, an increase in the cap has the potential to accelerate the rate of lending by credit unions if that legislation is enacted.

Lending by Nondepository Sources

In this changing financial marketplace, small businesses have been diversifying their providers of financial services. Nondepository institutions have become increasingly important sources of financial services to small businesses. According to the 1998 and 2003 SSBFs, while two-fifths of firms reported using at least one nondepository source for their financial services in 1998, more than one-half of them did so in 2003. However, firms reported receiving most of their credit products (lines of credit, loans, and capital leases) from depository sources. Among nondepository sources, finance companies were the primary provider of credit.[60]

More recently, small firms are turning to alternative nondepository sources for credit products. While a growing share of firms interviewed in the 1998 and 2003 SSBFs indicated using nondepository institutions, less than 2 percent reported that such institutions were their primary source for financial products. The 2009 NFIB survey reported a similar share of businesses using something other than a bank, credit union, or savings and loan as their primary financial institution. This share more than doubled by 2011, when 5.0 percent of firms reported having a nondepository primary institution. In addition, firms may receive credit from institutions that are not their primary financial institution, likely making the shares of firms reporting them as a primary institution a lower bound for their total usage. While the fraction of total loans in this category is relatively small, the fact that it is increasing indicates a growing need for this type of funding. While there are an ever-growing number of nondepository sources of financing, data are scarce. This section will briefly discuss finance company lending, venture capital funding, and crowdfunding and peer-to-peer lending.

Finance Companies

Businesses use finance companies primarily for the purchase of motor vehicles or other business equipment.[61] As with lending by commercial banks, lending by finance companies fell steeply between 2008 and 2009 (table 19). It is not possible to separate the data according to the size of the business, but given the size of the decline, it is safe to conclude that finance company lending to small and large businesses fell. Lending by finance companies has continued to decline through the first quarter of 2012.

Venture Capital

Venture capital provides funding to early-stage companies with potential for high growth. Venture capital funds make money by owning equity in the companies in which they invest. Investments by venture capital funds fell from about $30 billion in 2007 to $20 billion in 2009, but they have recovered somewhat since then and are on pace to reach $23 billion in 2012 (figure 9). Financing of firms at very early stages of development also declined in 2009 but rebounded in 2010 and 2011.

Peer-to-Peer Lending and Crowdfunding

Peer-to-peer lending allows individuals to lend money to other individuals without using a traditional financial institution. Since 2005, many peer-to-peer lending sites have been launched on the Internet to link potential borrowers to potential lenders. In 2008, the Securities and Exchange Commission (SEC) determined that peer-to-peer lending must be regulated as securities. As a result, businesses and major sites were shut down while participants attempted to get their sites registered with the SEC and reconfigure their platforms to conform to the new regulations. Since relaunching, lending volumes have steadily increased, boosted in part by the financial crisis and difficulties encountered by traditional financial institutions.[62]

Peer-to-peer lending sites have seen a dramatic increase in the number of loans over the past several years. Loan-level data provided by Prosper.com and LendingClub.com the largest peer-to-peer lending sites—indicate that dollar volume of peer-to-peer lending grew by nearly 300 percent between 2008 and 2011 (figure 10). The total dollars that went to small businesses has also been steadily increasing since 2009.[63]

Table 19. Outstanding loans to businesses by finance companies, 2007–12

Billions of dollars						
Category	**2007**	**2008**	**2009**	**2010**	**2011**	**2012: Q1**
Business	598.0	573.3	463.6	447.2	441.4	436.5
Motor vehicles	103.1	91.4	61.2	70.6	70.7	73.3
Retail loans	15.9	12.4	9.9	9.3	10.8	11.7
Wholesale loans[1]	56.0	49.2	35.6	46.2	44.5	46.0
Leases	31.2	29.8	15.7	15.1	15.3	15.6
Equipment	322.3	325.1	281.1	295.0	288.8	283.9
Loans	105.9	100.2	79.6	104.2	104.2	105.1
Leases	216.4	224.9	201.5	190.7	184.5	178.8
Other business receivables[2]	97.3	95.0	89.2	81.6	82.0	79.3
Securitized assets[3]	75.3	61.8	32.1	.0	.0	.0

Note: Data were revised June 2012.

[1] Credit arising from transactions between manufacturers and dealers—that is, floor plan financing.

[2] Outstanding balances of pools upon which securities have been issued; these balances are no longer carried on the balance sheets of the loan originator.

[3] Includes loans on commercial accounts receivable, factored commercial accounts, and receivable dealer capital; small loans used primarily for business or farm purposes; and wholesale and lease paper for mobile homes, recreation vehicles, and travel trailers.

Source: Federal Reserve Board, Statistical Release G.20, "Finance Companies."

Over the past four years, Lending Club and Prosper have been responsible for over $50 million in small business loans (table 20). For Prosper, business loans represent 16.1 percent of all dollars lent over this period; for Lending Club, business loans are only 5.6 percent of loan dollars. However, the average loans funded by Prosper have higher interest rates and are one-half to two-thirds the average loan funded by Lending Club. Although the total dollar volume is small relative to other sources, this high growth reflects the overall increase in all types of Lending Club and Prosper loans and a rapidly growing influence in this type of lending.

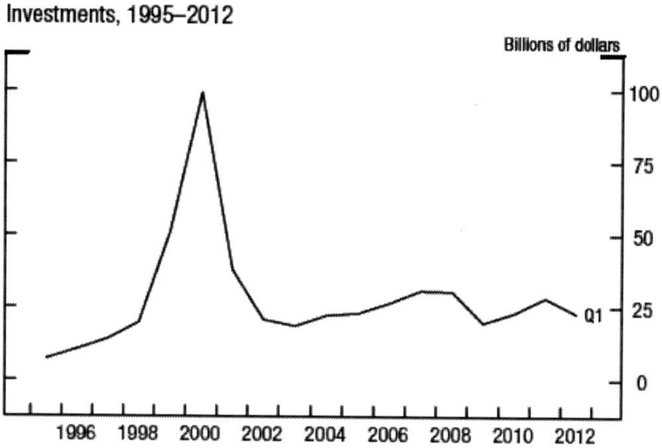

Amount and number of investments, 2007–12						
Development stage	**2007**	**2008**	**2009**	**2010**	**2011**	**2012:Q1**
Venture capital						
Investments (billions of dollars)	30.8	30.5	19.7	23.3	28.4	23.0
Number of deals	4,124	4,111	3,065	3,526	3,673	3,032
Average deal size (millions of dollars)	7.5	7.4	6.4	6.6	7.7	7.6
Seed, start-up, early stage						
Investments (billions of dollars)	7.6	7.2	6.6	7.4	9.2	7.0
Number of deals	1,603	1,632	1,312	1,617	1,810	1,372
Average deal size (millions of dollars)	4.7	4.4	5.0	4.5	5.1	5.1

Note: Data are at an annual rate.

Source: PricewaterhouseCoopers National Venture Capital Association Money Tree Report.

Figure 9. Venture capital.

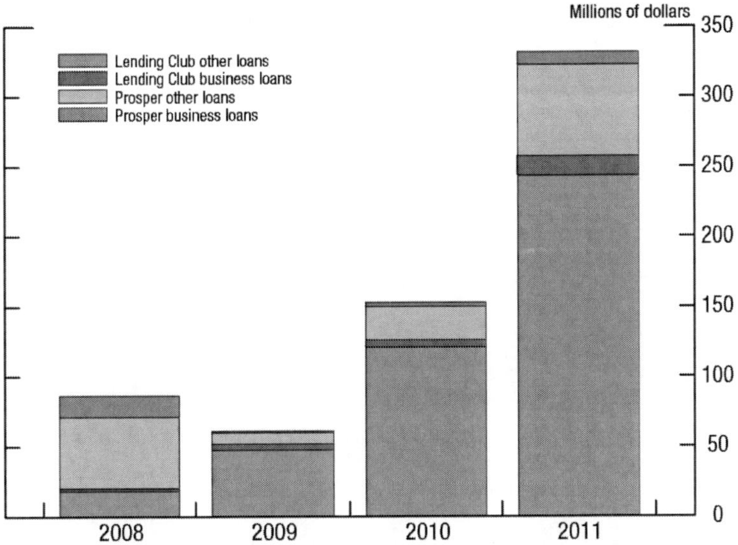

Source: Calculations from individual loan data from LendingClub.com and Prosper. com (see www.lendingclub.com/info/download-data.action and www. prosper. com/tools/DataExport.aspx).

Figure 10. Peer-to-peer loans funded, 2008–11.

On a final note, both sites also provide some information on loans that were not funded. The data indicate that there were over $600 million in requests for business loans over this four-year period that were not funded, nearly $400 million in 2011 alone. This unmet demand suggests that as the economy began to improve and standards at commercial banks were still relatively tight, small businesses began searching for alternative sources of finance.

Similar to peer-to-peer lending, many crowdfunding sites have surfaced online. Crowdfunding involves large numbers of people purchasing small equity stakes in the firm. However, the legality of sites such as Kiva, MicroPlace, Indiegogo, and Kickstarter has come into question, and it has been argued that such sites should be registered as broker dealers to facilitate the selling of shares in order to minimize fraudulent offerings. In early April of 2012, the Jumpstart Our Business Startups (JOBS) Act was signed into law; it creates a crowdfunding exemption from SEC regulations for firms raising less than $2 million, but with limits on individual investments. Due to the act's recent passage, data are not yet available on the extent to which small businesses use crowdfunding sources to raise capital.

Table 20. Small business lending by Prosper and Lending Club, 2008–11

Lender and year	Number of loans	Dollar amount funded	Average dollar amount funded	Average interest rate
Prosper				
2008	1,714	15,240,122	8,892	17.6
2009	212	1,165,140	5,496	18.4
2010	550	3,092,768	5,623	20.3
2011	1,195	9,092,801	7,609	23.5
Lending Club				
2008	127	1,683,250	13,254	12.0
2009	358	4,392,125	11,935	14.6
2010	466	5,384,875	11,556	12.5
2011	975	13,861,950	14,217	13.1

Source: Prosper.com and LendingClub.com.

SPECIAL ISSUES

This section examines some developments in small business credit markets that have affected the delivery and availability of credit to small businesses and are likely to continue doing so: government initiatives to support credit access for small businesses, securitiza-tion of small business loans, and the role of personal wealth in new business formation. First, government initiatives such as the CRA and SBA lending programs are reviewed. These programs focus on the financing needs of small firms in underserved communities and the financing needs of young firms without much, or any, financial history. New legislation specifically targeted to improve small business access to credit that was passed during this period is also discussed. Second, the securitization market is examined. A well-functioning secondary market increases small businesses' access to credit by providing an efficient funding supplement to direct lending. The willingness of banks to make small business loans can be reduced if securitization markets seize up, as happened during the recent recession. Finally, the personal wealth effects of the large decline in home prices over the recent period may be reflected in borrowing difficulties of potential new firms; the final part looks at the relationship between the recent decline in real estate prices and new business formation.

Government Initiatives to Support Credit Access for Small Business

Several long-standing government initiatives exist to help support credit access for small businesses, particularly small businesses owned by historically underserved groups such as women and minorities. Two such initiatives of particular importance are the CRA and several loan programs sponsored by the SBA.

Community Reinvestment Act

The Congress enacted the CRA in 1977 to encourage federally insured depository institutions to help meet the credit needs of their local communities, particularly low- and moderate-income (LMI) neighborhoods, consistent with safe and sound operations. These local communities, referred to hereafter as CRA assessment areas, are generally identified as the areas where banking institutions have a physical branch office presence and take deposits. LMI neighborhoods have been defined for regulatory purposes as census tracts with a median family income of less than 80 percent of the median family income of the broader area according to decennial census data.[64]

Under the CRA, the bank regulatory agencies regularly review institutions' performance in this endeavor and prepare publicly available written evaluations, which include ratings. The CRA requires that supervisory agencies consider a financial institution's CRA performance when evaluating an institution's application for expansion or relocation of depository facilities through branching, mergers, or acquisitions. Decisions on these applications are made public.

Although much of the small business lending of financial institutions occurring in LMI areas cannot be directly attributed to the CRA, bankers and community representatives indicate that some of it is the result of individual banks responding to their CRA obligation. Some lending activity also results from interaction with community representatives and government agencies familiar with the CRA and the possible roles that financial institutions can play in community development and reinvestment.

A common type of community reinvestment intermediary used by banks to help finance small businesses in lower-income areas is the bank-owned or bank-affiliated community development corporation. Under certain conditions, bank holding companies, national- and state-chartered commercial banks, and savings institutions may make equity investments in small businesses through a community development corporation or a limited liability company.

Generally, these entities can make debt and equity investments in small businesses when the firms are located in LMI areas and the jobs created and services provided benefit primarily LMI persons.

Another form of intermediary is the consortium lending organization that specializes in financing young or start-up small and minority businesses. By participating in such consortiums, banks can mitigate the risks and costs of lending to small firms. These loan consortiums are usually organized in corporate form and may be nonprofit or for-profit organizations. Although many are organized primarily by banks, they often have nonbank participants such as insurance companies, utilities, other corporations, religious institutions, and other institutional investors. Other loan consortiums are quasi-public arms of state, regional, or local governments.

Because many institutions do not have the expertise or cannot bear the development costs of special small business finance programs, especially those focusing on reinvestment areas, many banks have created or assisted intermediaries that support small businesses in their communities. Indeed, a notable development in bank reinvestment programs has been formal and informal working partnerships among banks, regional or neighborhood nonprofit organizations, and community-based development corporations. These organizations identify prospective borrowers, provide loan counseling, serve as experienced developers in low-income and minority areas, and assist banks in marketing loan programs. One such program is based in Philadelphia, where five major banks started a 2010 Capacity Building Initiative to increase the ability of FINANTA, a community development financial institution lender in Northeast Philadelphia, to grant loans and provide technical assistance to small businesses in underserved areas. This initiative provided critical resources to FINANTA in the forms of operating grants, technical assistance, loan capital, and loan loss reserve funds. Following the success of this initiative, the local banks will seek to provide assistance to another community lending partner in 2013. These types of partnerships have also been effective in helping reduce the high transaction costs often associated with lending to very small firms. Such organizations also frequently package financial resources for small firms from several public and private sources. Overall, these types of partnerships enable banks to make small business loans that might not otherwise have been financially feasible.

Analysis of Community Reinvestment Act Data on Lending in Lower-Income and Minority Neighborhoods

CRA regulations require larger commercial banks and savings associations to collect and report data regarding the geographic location of their small business lending. As a consequence of amendments to CRA regulations in 2005, banking institutions with assets less than $1.16 billion are no longer required to report data on their small business and small farm lending. However, many smaller institutions still elect to report these data. Analysis of Call Report data indicates that lenders reporting CRA data account for over two-thirds of the dollar volume of small business loans outstanding at all commercial banks and savings associations.

Each reporting bank makes an annual report on the total number and dollar volume of small business loan originations by census tract. As in the Call Report data, small business loans encompass C&I loans and CRE loans whose original amounts are $1 million or less. However, unlike the Call Report data, the CRA data provide information on originations, or the *flow*, of small business credit rather than the *stock*.[65] The CRA data also provide information on the number and dollar volume of small business loans originated to businesses with revenues of less than $1 million, to the extent that the reporting institution collects such information when making credit decisions.

Figure 11, panel A, shows that the dollar volume of small business loan originations peaked in 2007 and declined sharply thereafter, falling about 45 percent by 2010, the latest year for which data are available. Originations to the smallest businesses dropped more than 50 percent between 2007 and 2010. Panels B and C disaggregate these two series by whether loans were made in a bank's CRA assessment area and whether loans were made in LMI neighborhoods (see previous section for assessment area and LMI definitions).

Although the decline within assessment areas has been considerable, both panels show a more precipitous decline in small business loan origination volume outside of assessment areas. The downturn in lending has been similar across LMI and non-LMI neighborhoods inside and outside of assessment areas, suggesting that small business credit access in lower-income areas has not worsened disproportionately relative to upper-income neighborhoods.

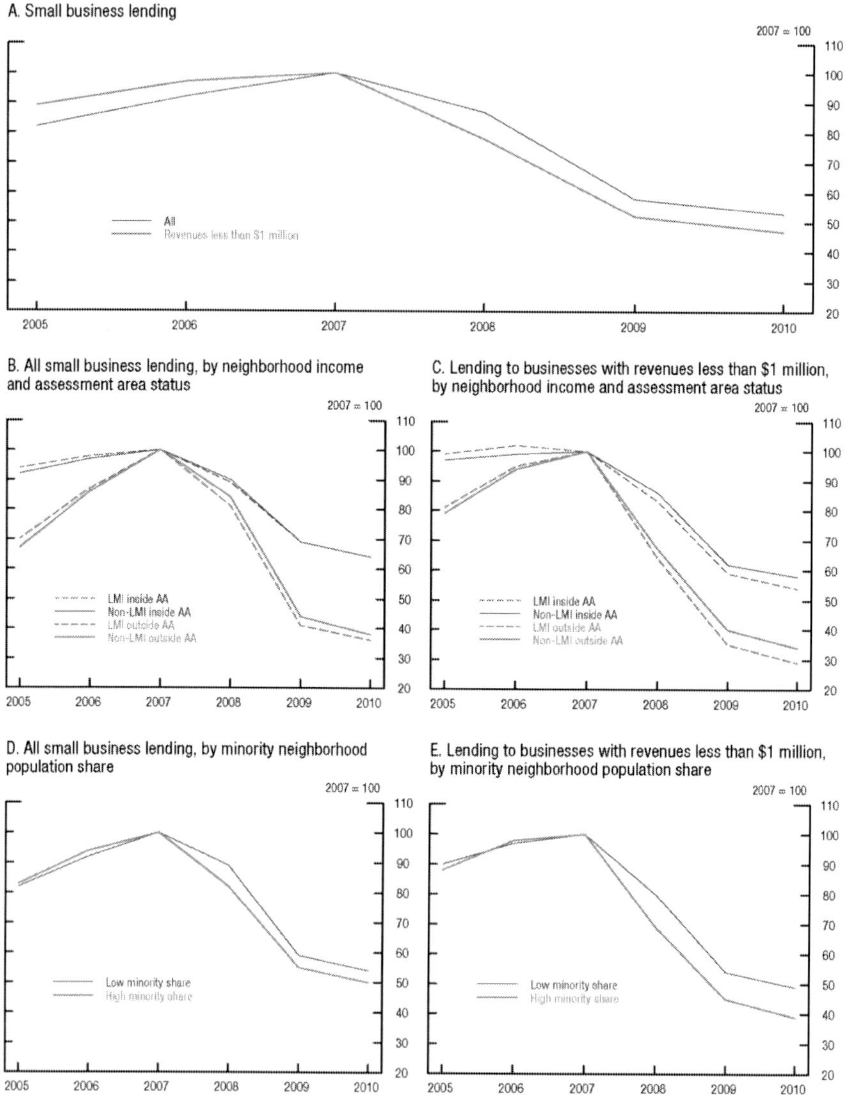

Note: LMI is low and moderate income; AA is assessment area.

Source: Federal Financial Institutions Examination Council, data reported under the Community Reinvestment Act.

Figure 11. Community reinvestment, 2005–10.

Panels D and E display the trend in lending across neighborhoods with higher (at least 30 percent) and lower (less than 30 percent) shares of minority residents. Since 2007, small business lending has declined somewhat more in higher-minority-share neighborhoods. The difference is more pronounced for loans to the smallest businesses those businesses with revenues less than $1 million. Lending in higher-minority-share neighborhoods has dropped about 60 percent since 2007, compared with a drop of roughly 50 percent in lower-minority-share neighborhoods.

Table 21 provides additional data on small business lending in LMI versus non-LMI neighborhoods, and inside versus outside of CRA assessment areas. The top panel shows data for 2007, while the bottom panel shows data for 2010. Comparing across columns, the volume of lending is considerably higher in non-LMI neighborhoods than in LMI neighborhoods in both years, reflecting, at least in part, that roughly three-fourths of the population and businesses reside in non-LMI neighborhoods.

Within each income group, assessment area lending generally exceeds non assessment area lending in dollar terms, but not in terms of the number of loans. This pattern results from specialized credit card lending institutions making up a large portion of non assessment area lending. A dozen or so such institutions issue business cards nationwide but generally do not have an extensive network of bank branches and therefore have limited CRA assessment areas.[66] Comparing LMI with non-LMI areas, table 21 indicates that credit card lenders made up a larger share of loan origination volume in non-LMI areas than in LMI areas in both 2007 (25.5 percent versus 19.4 percent) and 2010 (10.6 percent versus 8.0 percent).

Finally, table 21 also shows the share of small business lending by banks in the top 10 banking organizations according to total assets, by neighborhood income group. These data reveal that the top 10 organizations accounted for just over one-third of dollars loaned in both LMI and non-LMI neighborhoods in 2007 and for just under one-third of lending in both tract groups in 2010.[67]

Small Business Administration Programs

Support for small business development has been a priority of policymakers for several decades, and federal, state, and local agencies have sponsored programs that assist in channeling capital to small business. At the federal level, the agency with the most direct role in this objective is the SBA, which the Congress created in 1953 to help entrepreneurs form successful small enterprises. The SBA provides financing to young and growing small firms through several channels such as the 7(a) Loan Program and SBA 504 Certified Development Companies (CDCs). Among the policy objectives of the SBA loan programs are the goals of promoting entrepreneurship opportunities for women and minorities.

SBA 7(a) Loan Program

The largest SBA program is the 7(a) Loan Program, which provides lenders with a partial loan guarantee for extending credit to small businesses that meet the SBA's underwriting and eligibility criteria. Participating lenders agree to structure loans according to the SBA's requirements, and apply for and receive a guarantee from the SBA on a portion of this loan. The SBA does not fully guarantee 7(a) loans the lender and the SBA share the risk that a borrower will not be able to repay the loan in full. The SBA provides a guarantee of as much as 85 percent for loans less than or equal to $150,000 and a guarantee of as much as 75 percent for loans greater than $150,000.[68] The maximum loan amount is now generally $5 million, increased in 2010 from $2 million under the Small Business Jobs Act of 2010. However, under the Express loan program, which requires less loan documentation and provides quicker turnaround time, only 50 percent of the loan is guaranteed, and the maximum loan amount is $500,000.

Figure 12, panel A, shows that although the dollar volume of SBA 7(a) loans jumped dramatically between 2009 and 2011, with gross loan approvals increasing from about $9 billion to nearly $20 billion, the number of loans has remained at subdued levels relative to 2007 and earlier. Thus, the average 7(a) loan size has increased sharply, especially from 2010 to 2011, which may partly reflect increases in the maximum loan size allowed.

Panel B shows time trends in the fraction of 7(a) loans reported to have gone to minority- and women-owned businesses, and the fraction of loans below $150,000, which qualify for a larger guarantee percentage and are more likely to have gone to smaller businesses. The share of loans to women-owned businesses has declined somewhat from 23.0 percent in 2007 and 2008 to 16.7 percent in 2011, while the share of loans to minority-owned businesses has declined more noticeably from 34.3 percent in 2007 to 21.4 percent in 2011. This panel also shows that the fraction of loans under $150,000 has been declining steadily since 2007.

Table 21. Small business lending, by neighborhood income and assessment area status, 2007 and 2010

Category	LMI			Non-LMI			Total[1]
	Inside AA	Outside AA	Total	Inside AA	Outside AA	Total	
2007							
Small business loans							
Dollar volume (millions)	45,463	21,645	67,108	144,246	111,089	255,335	325,774
Share by credit card lender (percent)	1.8	56.2	19.4	1.9	56.2	25.5	24.1
Share by top 10 bank organizations (percent)	32.2	39.5	34.6	31.2	39.5	34.8	35.2
Number of loans (thousands)	468	1,943	2,411	1,674	9,065	10,739	13,284
Average loan amount (thousands)	97.1	11.1	27.8	86.2	12.3	23.8	24.5
Loans to businesses with revenues less than $1 Million							
Dollar volume (millions)	16,645	8,966	25,611	61,205	48,307	109,512	136,411
Share of all (percent)	37.0	41.0	38.0	42.0	43.0	43.0	42.0
Share by credit card lender (percent)	3.8	52.5	20.8	3.1	50.8	24.1	23.3
Share by top 10 bank organizations (percent)	31.7	43.6	35.9	30.6	39.1	34.3	35.1
Number of loans (thousands)	275	632	907	1,071	3,055	4,126	5,081
Average loan amount (thousands)	60.5	14.2	28.2	57.1	15.8	26.5	26.8
2010							
Small business loans							
Dollar volume (millions)	29,026	7,825	36,851	92,006	42,629	134,635	174,817
Share by credit card lender (percent)	.1	37.2	8.0	.1	33.5	10.6	10.1
Share by top 10 bank organizations (percent)	30.8	32.4	31.2	30.7	32.0	31.1	31.9
Number of loans (thousands)	248	480	728	933	2,421	3,354	4,216
Average loan amount (thousands)	117.0	16.3	50.6	98.6	17.6	40.1	41.5

Table 21. (Continued)

Category	LMI			Non-LMI			Total[1]
	Inside AA	Outside AA	Total	Inside AA	Outside AA	Total	
Loans to businesses with revenues less than $1 million							
Dollar volume (millions)	9,043	2,556	11,599	35,425	16,267	51,692	64,579
Share of all (percent)	31.0	33.0	31.0	39.0	38.0	38.0	37.0
Share by credit card lender (percent)	.0	22.8	5.0	.0	19.5	6.1	5.9
Share by top 10 bank organizations (percent)	28.4	38.5	30.6	30.5	34.8	31.9	32.7
Number of loans (thousands)	132	114	246	570	625	1,195	1,489
Average loan amount (thousands)	68.5	22.4	47.2	62.1	26.0	43.3	43.4

Note: LMI is low and moderate income; AA is assessment area.

[1] Includes lending with unknown income and assessment area status.

Source: Federal Financial Institutions Examination Council, data reported under the Community Reinvestment Act.

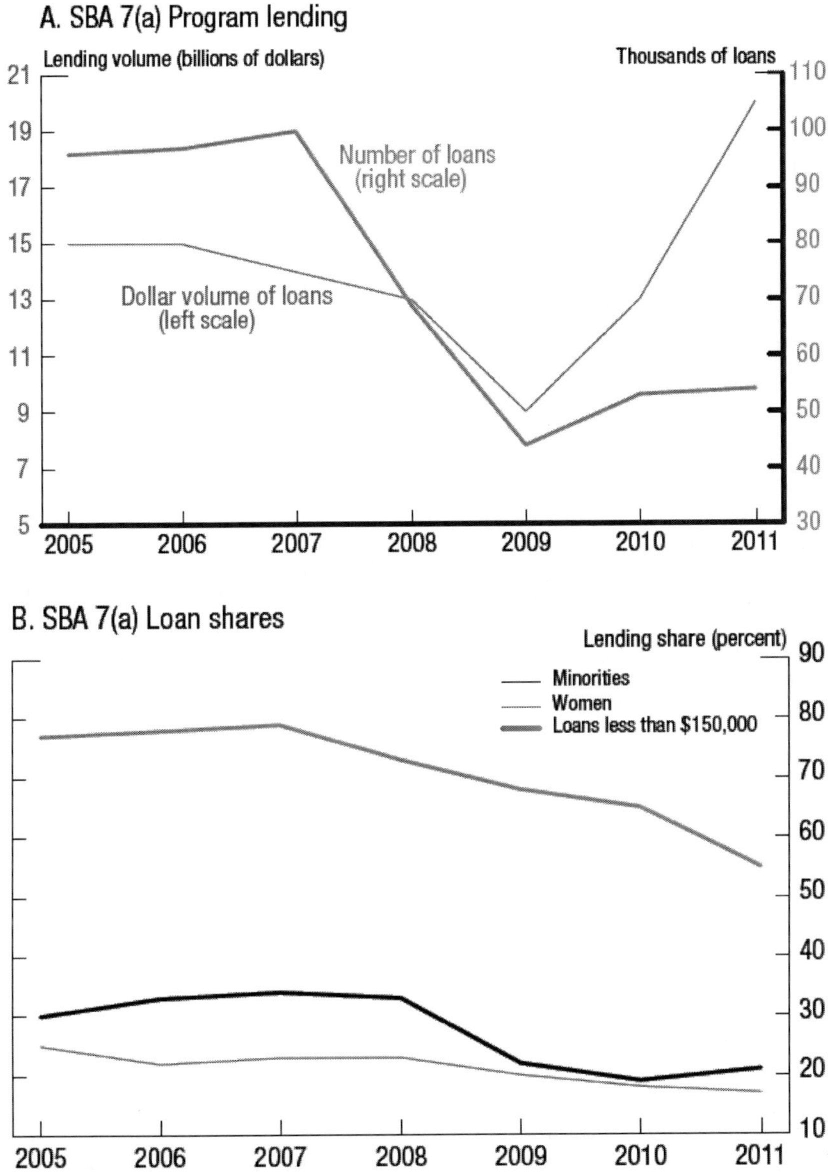

Note: SBA is Small Business Administration.

Source: For panel A, Small Business Administration; for panel B, National Association of Government Guaranteed Lenders.

Figure 12. Small Business Administration 7(a) Program, 2005–11.

SBA 504 Certified Development Companies

Banks often work with CDCs to leverage funds for small business financing. CDCs are generally nonprofit corporations specializing in small business finance and are certified by the SBA to participate in the agency's section 504 financing program. The SBA 504 program is intended to help small businesses expand and to create jobs by providing CDCs with the ability to issue SBA-guaranteed long-term debentures to fund small firms' purchase of plant, equipment, or real estate. These loans are typically structured with three components: (1) a first mortgage or lien, which is made by a private commercial lender for 50 percent of the total project and does not come with a government guarantee; (2) a second mortgage or lien, which is made by a CDC for 40 percent of the total project and is backed by a 100 percent SBA-guaranteed debenture; and (3) borrower equity for the remaining 10 percent of the total project. SBA 504 loan volume peaked in 2007 with about $6.5 billion in gross 11approvals. Lending under this program in fiscal year 2011 was at $4.6 billion in gross approvals on 7,676 loans, similar to the level in 2010 and about 18 percent higher than in 2009.

In 2011, the 504 program was temporarily changed to allow small business owners to use 504 loans to refinance up to 90 percent of the appraised value of available collateral. This temporary expansion authorizes up to $7.5 billion in financing and is available until September 27, 2012.

Small Business Investment Companies

The Small Business Investment Company (SBIC) program was initiated in 1957 to provide debt and equity capital to young and growing companies. Although the venture capital market has matured, the SBIC program remains important because many small, growing firms find it difficult to obtain equity financing from venture capital companies. Banks and bank holding companies can own and operate SBICs, which are licensed and regulated by the SBA. SBICs can be organized as separate subsidiaries of one institution, or of multiple institutions and other private investors, or can be controlled by private interests not affiliated with financial institutions. To obtain capital, SBICs often sell long-term debentures that are guaranteed by the SBA. The proceeds of these debentures are used to provide longer-term financing for small businesses, often in conjunction with the issuance of equity interests in the small business to the SBIC. In fiscal 2011, SBICs provided $2.6 billion of financing to small businesses. This figure represents an increase of more than 60 percent over the $1.6 billion from fiscal 2010 and well above the $1.3 billion averaged between 2006 and 2009.

Disaster Recovery Assistance

The SBA has a long-standing program to assist businesses recovering from disasters. In fiscal 2007, the SBA funded just over 1,400 loans totaling nearly $14 billion for this purpose. A significant portion of the demand in fiscal 2007 stemmed from Gulf Coast hurricanes in 2005. In fiscal 2008, the SBA funded just over 15,000 loans totaling just over $800 million for this purpose. Severe tornadoes and flooding in the Midwest and tropical storms and hurricanes in the Southeast, along the Atlantic coast, account for a large part of those damages. In fiscal 2009, the SBA funded over 21,000 loans totaling $1.1 billion for this purpose. Damages caused by Hurricanes Ike and Gustav and the flooding in the Midwest were responsible for many of these loans. In fiscal 2010, the SBA funded almost 14,000 loans totaling nearly $600 million for this purpose. The largest component of these loans stems from damages sustained during the flooding in Tennessee, Rhode Island, and Massachusetts and the BP oil spill. In fiscal 2011, the SBA funded 13,643 loans totaling $739 million for this purpose. During fiscal 2011, nearly 14,000 loans were made, totaling about $783 million. These loans were mainly associated with damages caused by tornadoes in Alabama and Missouri and flooding in North Dakota, as well as Hurricane Irene.

Microloan Program

The SBA's Microloan Program provides small businesses with small short-term loans for working capital or the purchase of inventory, supplies, furniture, fixtures, machinery, or equipment. The SBA makes funds available to specially designated intermediary lenders, which are nonprofit community-based organizations with experience in lending as well as management and technical assistance. These intermediaries make loans to eligible borrowers. The maximum loan amount is $50,000, but the average microloan is about $13,000. In fiscal 2012, the SBA budgeted $3.8 million to support the Microloan Program.

Small Business Credit Access Legislation

Support for small businesses has recently come in the form of more-significant small business legislation. The American Recovery and Reinvestment Act of 2009 (ARRA) and the Small Business Jobs Act of 2010 both provided resources to small businesses through increasing credit availability, providing capital to small business lenders, and putting in place tax cuts for small businesses.

American Recovery and Reinvestment Act of 2009

With the overarching goal of spurring job creation, ARRA included some specific provisions directly targeted at small businesses, including increased small business financing as well as tax breaks. The increased financing was implemented in the form of funding for the SBA, which received $730 million, more than doubling its 2008 budget. The funds were divided among many programs, with $375 million for temporarily eliminating fees on SBA-backed loans and raising the guarantee percentages, up from the 75 percent maximum to 90 percent on some loans.

Another $255 million was used to create the America's Recovery Capital (ARC) Loan Program. ARC loans were designated to help businesses in distress pay off existing debt, and could be a maximum of $35,000.[69]

The SBA ran out of funding to waive fees and raise guarantee percentages in late November of 2009, but the next month the Senate extended the funding, allotting another $125 million to continue the program until February 2010. Other components were less successful. The SBA estimated that the $255 million appropriated for the ARC program would lead to 10,000 loans worth $340 million, but by the time the program expired at the end of September 2010, only 8,869 loans worth $287 million had been made. Anecdotally, small businesses expressed desire to participate in the program but cited cumbersome paperwork and banks' unwillingness to cooperate as hindering their ability to receive an ARC loan.[70]

Small Business Jobs Act of 2010

In September 2010, the Small Business Jobs Act was signed into law. This act again provided funding for the SBA and expanded small business tax cuts, as well as authorized the creation of the Small Business Lending Fund (SBLF) of the Treasury Department, with the aim of increasing the availability of credit for small businesses. A $505 million subsidy for the SBA supported over $12 billion in small business lending and allowed the SBA to increase maximum sizes in several of its loan programs. Employment and revenue size standards were also raised, increasing the amount of small businesses eligible for SBA loans. According to self-reported data, Small Business Jobs Act loans went to rural (22 percent), minority-owned (21 percent), women-owned (16 percent), and veteran-owned (7 percent) businesses.[71] The SBLF was created to encourage lending to small businesses by providing capital to community banks and community development loan funds (CDLFs) with assets under $10 billion. The fund was supplied with $30 billion but in total provided just over $4 billion to 332 community banks and CDLFs. In April 2012, the Treasury reported that institutions that received capital from the SBLF significantly increased small business lending in 2011, with $1.3 billion more lent in the fourth quarter than in the third quarter and a total of $4.8 billion more lent over the 2010 average.[72]

In addition, the Act created the State Small Business Credit Initiative (SSBCI), which was funded with $1.5 billion to strengthen state programs that support lending to small businesses and small manufacturers. Under the SSBCI, participating states will use the federal funds for programs that leverage private lending to help finance small businesses and manufacturers that are creditworthy, but are not getting the loans they need to expand and create jobs.

Jumpstart Our Business Startups Act

The most recent piece of small business legislation is the JOBS Act. Signed into law in early April of 2012, this bill is intended to make it easier for start-ups and small businesses to raise funds, especially through crowdfunding online. This legislation is a departure from the two earlier bills, as it is focused on access to finance through less conventional channels.[73]

Securitization of Small Business Loans

The securitization of small business loans has the potential to substantially influence the availability of credit to small businesses. Potential benefits exist for lenders, borrowers, and investors. However, the obstacles to securitizing small business loans are large. Between 2002 and 2007, securitization of SBA loans increased at a moderate pace each fiscal year. Then, in late 2008, the securitization markets nearly collapsed. Unable to sell their loans in the secondary market, banks that relied on selling asset-backed securities (ABS) packages to provide them with additional lending funds were forced to pull back on their lending. Outstanding business loans fell substantially through the second quarter of 2010 and recovered to near pre-recession levels by the fourth quarter of 2011. Outstanding small loans to businesses began increasing only in the fourth quarter of 2011 and remain nearly 15 percent below pre-recession levels.[74]

Process of Securitization

Securitization is the process of packaging individual loans and other debt instruments, converting the package into a security, and enhancing the credit status or rating to further the security's sale to third-party investors (Kendall and Fishman, 1998). This process has become an efficient funding supplement to direct lending in markets for certain financial assets—notably, residential mortgages, credit card receivables, and automobile loans.

Active secondary markets in these assets can benefit all parties. Lenders profit from scale economies or from originating and servicing loans without having to add all of the loans to their own balance sheets. They can therefore improve their return on capital by substituting off-balance-sheet, fee-based sources of income for riskier capital-intensive direct lending. This practice potentially results in added liquidity and greater balance sheet diversity. Borrowers whose loans are eligible for securitization typically enjoy lower financing costs. Investors in the securities, while still earning attractive returns, may receive greater liquidity and lower risk than they would by investing directly in the individual loans. Overall, risk may be allocated more efficiently.

Successful securitization requires that the costs of pooling individual loans and administering the securities collateralized by the loans be less than the spread between the average contract rate on the underlying loans and the yield investors demand on the securities. Besides various expenses for administration, costs stem from obtaining a high credit rating to reassure investors of the reliability of a security's cash flow. High ratings are often obtained through the provision of "credit enhancements" to the security's purchaser by the originator or others. These enhancements sometimes involve an agreement by the originator or other party to absorb, through the portion of the pool held by them, specified first dollar losses of the pool before any loss falls on the investors in the securitized pool.

Securitization generally has thrived in markets in which the costs of acquiring and communicating information to investors about loans and borrowers are low. These conditions usually occur as a result of standardized loan underwriting criteria; advances in information technology, which make estimating default probabilities and prepayment patterns easier under various economic conditions; and experience in developing and selling loan pools in the secondary market. Most small business loans cannot readily be grouped into large pools that credit agencies and investors can easily analyze: Loan terms and conditions are not homogeneous, underwriting standards vary across originators, and information on historical loss rates is typically limited. The information problems associated with small business loans can be overcome, or offset to a degree, by some form of credit enhancement, as in the case of the SBA's 7(a) loans. However, the more loss protection needed to sell the securities, the smaller are both the net proceeds from the sale of the securities and the incentive for lenders to securitize their loans. Small business loans are an asset for which the high transaction costs of providing credit enhancements have made many potential securitizations unprofitable.

A significant step in encouraging the development of markets for securitized small business loans has been the removal of certain regulatory impediments. The Riegle Community Development and Regulatory Improvement Act of 1994 (Riegle Act) extended some of the regulatory accommodation provided by the Secondary Mortgage Market Enhancement Act of 1984 to issuers of securities backed by small business loans (and commercial mortgages). The 1984 act applied only to issuers of residential mortgage-backed securities. The benefits of the Riegle Act include the elimination of state-level investment restrictions and securities registration requirements as well as the establishment of favorable federal regulatory treatment. Investment restrictions for federally regulated banks, thrifts, and credit unions and for state-chartered thrifts, insurance companies, and pension funds were relaxed as well. Also, risk-based capital requirements for depository institutions that secu-ritize loans but retain "recourse" on subordinated classes of securities were reduced.

A remaining impediment to the development of markets for securitized small business loans has been the lack of more-uniform standards for underwriting and loan documentation. However, the use of credit-scoring systems in the origination of small business loans could address this problem, at least to some extent, by providing a credible, low-cost measure of the expected performance of small business loans. As a result, the information gap associated with small business lending could be lessened, and the volume of securitizations could increase. To date, however, this practice has not been broadly adopted.[75]

Securitization Activity

By 2006, new secondary-market dollar volume for 7(a) loans had risen to a record high of $4.6 billion. Conventional, non-SBA-secured small business loan securitizations were growing at a moderate pace, although at a much smaller rate than that of SBA-backed loans. In late 2008, the secondary market for small business loans slowed substantially. The top two issuers of small business loan ABS Lehman Brothers Small Business Finance and Ciena Capital—both filed for bankruptcy earlier in the year. In addition, Bayview Financial, another large player in the market, closed down its securitization operations in 2008.

SBA 7(a) Loans

Historically, most of the small business loans that have been securitized involved the guaranteed portion of loans made under the SBA's 7(a) Loan Program. These securitizations have been fairly common because they do not involve the risk and information impediments typically associated with the securitiza-tion of small business loans. SBA 7(a) loans tend to be highly standardized because the underlying loans are often backed by similar types of collateral and loan documentation. In addition, the originators are SBA "preferred lenders" and are perceived to have clear and rigorous underwriting standards that are consistently applied. Despite this preferred status, the SBA secondary market also dropped off substantially in September 2008.

As the secondary markets froze and regulators attempted to restore financial stability, several actions were undertaken, with important implications for the SBA 7(a) secondary market:

November 2008. As financial markets became more globalized, increasing shares of SBA lenders' cost of funds became tied to the London interbank offered rate (LIBOR). In a more stable financial environment, the LIBOR was consistently 3 percentage points lower than the prime rate, which was the rate required to price 7(a) loans. However, as the financial markets became increasingly volatile, the spread was reduced, thereby reducing the profitability of SBA loans. This reduction in turn led to increased difficulty in selling the loans on the secondary market. In order to reduce some of the risk and uncertainty to lenders, the SBA began allowing lenders to price loans based on the LIBOR rather than requiring the prime rate (U.S. Small Business Administration, 2008a). Around the same time, the SBA also announced that it would allow weighted-average coupon pools in order to make the SBA pools more attractive and more consistent with other types of securities sold on the secondary market (U.S. Small Business Administration, 2008b).

2008–09. The Federal Reserve established the Term Asset-Backed Securities Loan Facility (TALF) to increase credit availability and support economic activity by facilitating renewed issuance of consumer and small business ABS at more-normal interest rate spreads. The facility was announced on November 25, 2008, and began lending operations in March 2009. TALF lending was authorized through June 30, 2010, for loans collateralized by newly issued commercial mortgage-backed securities and through March 31, 2010, for loans collateralized by all other TALF-eligible securities.[76] Between March 2009 and June 2010, the Federal Reserve lent a total of $71.1 billion, $2.2 billion of which went toward SBA loans.

June 2009. The Financial Accounting Standards Board announced two new provisions (Statements of Financial Accounting Standards Nos. 166 and 167) intended to provide increased transparency for investors about a company's risks. In effect, the new provisions required that banks that sold the guaranteed portion of their 7(a) loans on the secondary market have to defer recognizing the income until after the 90-day warranty period required by the SBA. In addition, regulatory capital must be held until the sale can be recognized. Banks argued that these requirements made the income from servicing the loan more attractive than reselling it and reduced secondary market sales. In January 2011, the SBA removed the 90-day recourse period from the standard secondary-market agreement, allowing banks to recognize the income when the sale occurs.

As seen in figure 13, the secondary market for SBA 7(a) loans experienced a great deal of volatility over the past five years. Prior to September 2008, an average of $328 million settled in the secondary market each month. Between October 2008 and May 2009, less than $200 million settled each month. By mid-2009, average monthly settlements had returned to their previous levels. Settlements rose again throughout 2011, reflecting the record-high dollar volume of 7(a) loans approved with the increased funding from ARRA and the Small Business Jobs Act.

A similar pattern can be seen in looking at pricing premiums over this period. Because the guaranteed portion of the 7(a) loan is secured by the full faith and credit of the U.S. government, the loan is generally sold at a significant premium. During the peak of the crisis, a large fraction of the loans that were able to be resold in the secondary markets were sold at premiums at or below 103. By December 2009, the majority of loans were sold at or above a premium of 106—the prevailing premium level in 2007. Into 2010 and 2011, a growing portion of loans were being sold at or above a premium of 110, indicating investors' preference for a relatively low-risk asset.

Looking forward, the secondary market for 7(a) SBA loans appears to be healthy and operating well. With no programmatic changes in the foreseeable future, the market should continue to move along smoothly at current levels.

SBA 504 Loans

The other large loan program from the SBA is the 504 program, which primarily finances real estate. As noted earlier, 504 loans are typically funded through a combination of funds from a private lending institution, the SBA CDC, and the business owner. CDCs assist small business borrowers in preparing and submitting the SBA 504 loan applications. The debentures are packaged with other debentures into a national pool and sold monthly to investors. As the traditional markets become more volatile, the demand for these safe investments generally increases.

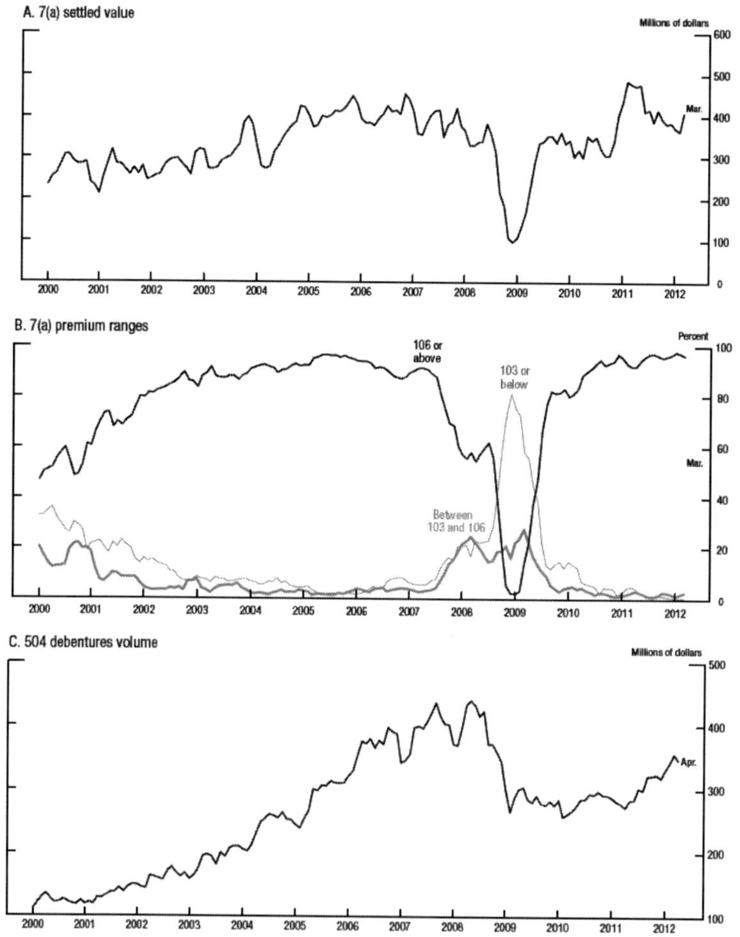

Note: Three-month moving average.

Source: Data provided by Small Business Administration, Office of Financial Assistance.

Figure 13. Small Business Administration secondary market, 2000–12.

As a provision of ARRA, a new program was created to encourage sales into the secondary market of the "first mortgage" portion of 504 loans. Under the new program, portions of eligible 504 first mortgages pooled by originators or broker dealers could be sold with an SBA guarantee to third-party investors in the secondary market. Lenders will retain at least 15 percent of each individual loan, pool originators will assume 5 percent of the risk, and the SBA will guarantee the remaining 80 percent. To be eligible to be included in a pool, the first mortgage must be associated with a 504 loan disbursed on or after February 17, 2009.

As seen in panel C of figure 13, the secondary volume for 504 debentures dropped off significantly in late 2008. It remained relatively flat throughout 2009 and 2010. Since 2011, it has been rapidly climbing but has not yet reached its peak level of 2007 08. With the first mortgage program, volumes are likely to increase throughout 2012 and then level out going forward.

Non-SBA Loans

With the bankruptcy of Lehman Brothers and Ciena Capital, new issuance of small business ABS not backed by an SBA guarantee has been quite limited since 2008. In its latest outlook for the small business loans ABS market, Moody's Investors Service forecasts that securitizations of these assets will remain "stressed" throughout 2012.[77]

Personal Wealth and New Business Formation

There is always a high degree of churning in the small business population, with firms going in and out of business. However, during the recent period, the rate of new business formation has declined. What has caused the lack of activity is not clear. There has been much speculation that the decline in home prices—and consequently home equity has constrained potential entrepreneurs' ability to finance a new business. However, existing business owners consistently report that lack of demand and economic uncertainty are the largest problems facing their business in recent periods, not access to capital.[78] The lack of demand, increased uncertainty, or both could have caused fewer business ideas to have a positive expected value and thus fewer businesses to be formed.

From a practical perspective, when starting a small business, entrepreneurs are faced with certain difficulties in obtaining the initial funding.

Due to the informational opacity surrounding young small businesses, obtaining start-up capital is often difficult. Without existing financial records for the firm, new businesses are generally not able to secure funding through traditional sources, and owners must often rely on personal savings and assets. It is difficult to obtain financial information from existing small businesses, but exponentially more so to get such information from businesses that were never established.

The financial history and resources of existing own-– ers becomes the only real source of credit information. Assuming that potential business owners are similar to existing owners, a small amount of data does exist. These data provide some evidence of the importance of personal wealth for start-ups. According to the Census Bureau's 2007 Survey of Business Owners, 62.0 percent of employer business owners reported tapping into their personal savings to start their businesses, and 8.3 percent reported using a home equity loan taken out against their personal residences (table 22). Among the most recently formed firms, personal savings and home equity were even more important, with 67.1 percent of firms using personal assets or savings and 12.4 percent using a home equity loan.

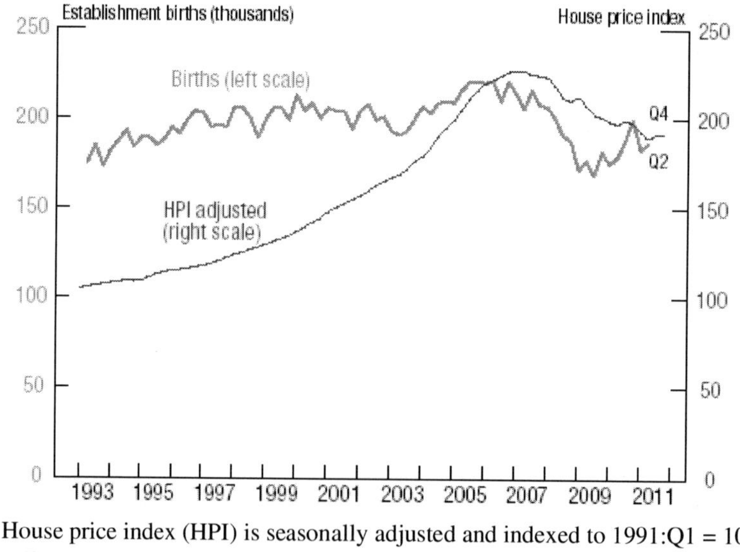

Note: House price index (HPI) is seasonally adjusted and indexed to 1991:Q1 = 100.
Source: For establishment births, Bureau of Labor Statistics; for house price index, Federal Housing Finance Agency.

Figure 14. Establishment births and house price index, 1993–2011.

Table 22. Source of start-up capital, by year of formation among employer firms, pre-1980 through 2007

Percent										
	Year business formed									
Source of start-up capital	**Before 1980**	**1980 to 1989**	**1990 to 1999**	**2000 to 2002**	**2003**	**2004**	**2005**	**2006**	**2007**	**All firms**
Personal/family savings of owner(s)	49.4	63.0	66.3	67.0	67.9	68.3	67.9	67.0	67.1	62.0
Personal/family assets other than savings of owner(s)	7.9	8.6	9.9	10.5	11.9	11.3	12.0	11.6	11.7	9.7
Personal/family home equity loan	4.7	6.0	7.6	10.0	12.6	12.9	14.0	13.6	12.4	8.3
Personal/business credit card(s)	2.9	6.6	11.9	15.3	17.3	16.1	17.1	17.0	16.5	10.5
Business loan from federal, state, or local government	1.3	1.2	1.3	1.4	1.4	1.3	1.5	1.2	1.3	1.3
Government-guaranteed business loan from a bank or financial institution	1.3	1.2	1.6	1.7	1.9	1.7	1.7	1.7	1.9	1.5
Business loan from a bank or financial institution	21.2	20.1	18.4	17.9	17.8	16.9	17.2	17.4	18.1	19.0
Business loan/investment from family/friends	5.5	4.5	4.4	4.5	4.6	4.7	4.9	4.7	4.9	4.8
Investment by venture capitalist(s)	.4	.5	.7	1.0	.9	1.1	1.1	1.4	1.3	.7
Grants	1.0	.8	.8	.8	.7	.6	.5	.6	.4	.8
Other source(s) of capital	4.2	2.9	3.3	3.7	3.8	3.9	4.0	4.5	5.2	3.7
Don't know	10.1	5.7	4.6	3.7	3.6	3.2	3.1	3.1	2.7	6.0
None needed	16.6	10.3	9.1	8.5	7.7	7.7	7.8		7.7	10.6

Note: Totals may sum to more than 100 because firms could indicate that multiple sources were used to start the firm.

†Estimate is withheld due to insufficient cell sizes.

Source: U.S. Census Bureau, special tabulation of the 2007 Survey of Business Owners.

To get a sense of how this reliance of new business owners on personal wealth and home equity played out over the recent period, figure 14 looks at the number of establishment births relative to overall home prices. As home prices increased, the number of establishments born in each period increased slightly. As home prices started to decrease, the number of establishments born each period decreased rapidly. While the data indicate that there is a positive relationship between housing wealth and business formation, it is not possible to determine the extent to which home price declines caused fewer businesses to be formed, as there are many other factors at play. However, it does seem likely that the home price declines had some effect on the level of firms established over the recent period.

REFERENCES

[1] Adams, Robert M. (2012). "*Consolidation and Merger Activity in the United States Banking Industry from 2000 through 2010*," Finance and Economics Discussion Series 2012-51. Washington: Board of Governors of the Federal Reserve System.

[2] Adams, Robert M. & Amel, Dean F. (2007). "*The Effects of Past Entry, Market Consolidation, and Expansion by Incumbents on the Probability of Entry*," Finance and Economics Discussion Series 2007-51. Washington: Board of Governors of the Federal Reserve System, July.

[3] Avery, Robert B. & Katherine Samolyk (2000). "*Bank Consolidation and the Provision of Banking Services: The Case of Small Commercial Loans*," Working Paper 00-1. Washington: Federal Deposit Insurance Corporation, December.

[4] —(2004). "Bank Consolidation and Small Business Lending: The Role of Community Banks," *Journal of Financial Services Research,* vol. *25* (April June), 291-325.

[5] Berger, Allen N., Bonime, Seth D., Goldberg, Lawrence G. & White, Lawrence J. (2004). "The Dynamics of Market Entry: The Effects of Mergers and Acquisitions on Entry in the Banking Industry," *Journal of Business,* vol. *77* (October), 797-834.

[6] Berger, Allen N., Demsetz, Rebecca S. & Strahan, Philip E. (1999). "The Consolidation of the Financial Services Industry: Causes, Consequences, and Implications for the Future," *Journal of Banking and Finance*, vol. *23* (February), 135-94.

[7] Berger, Allen N., Goldberg, Lawrence G. & White, Lawrence J. (2001). "The Effects of Dynamic Changes in Bank Competition on the Supply of Small Business Credit," *European Finance Review*, vol. *5* (1– 2), 115-39.

[8] Berger, Allen N., Rosen, Richard J. & Udell, Gregory F. (2001). "*The Effect of Market Size Structure on Competition: The Case of Small Business Lending*," Finance and Economics Discussion Series 2001-63. Washington: Board of Governors of the Federal Reserve System, December.

[9] Berger, Allen N., Anthony Saunders, Scalise, Joseph M. & Udell, Gregory F. (1998). "The Effects of Bank Mergers and Acquisitions on Small Business Lending," *Journal of Financial Economics,* vol. *50* (November), 187-229.

[10] Berger, Allen N. & Udell, Gregory F. (1998). "The Economics of Small Business Finance: The Roles of Private Equity and Debt Markets in the Financial Growth Cycle," *Journal of Banking and Finance*, vol. *22* (August), 613-73.

[11] —(2002). "Small Business Credit Availability and Relationship Lending: The Importance of Bank Organisational Structure," *Economic Journal*, vol. *112* (February), F32-F53.

[12] Bernanke, Ben S. (2010). "*Causes of the Recent Financial and Economic Crisis*," statement before the Financial Crisis Inquiry Commission, Washington, September 2, www.federalreserve.gov/ newsevents/ testimony/bernanke20100902a.htm.

[13] Bitler, Marianne P., Robb, Alicia M. & Wolken, John D. (2001). "Financial Services Used by Small –Businesses: Evidence from the 1998 Survey of Small Business Finances," *Federal Reserve Bulletin*, vol. *87* (April), 183-205.

[14] Board of Governors of the Federal Reserve System (2002). *Report to the Congress on the Availability of Credit to Small Businesses*. Washington: Board of Governors, September.

[15] —(2007). *Report to the Congress on the Availability of Credit to Small Businesses*. Washington: Board of Governors, October.

[16] Bogoslaw, David (2009). "Peer-to-Peer Lending: Problems and Promise." *Bloomberg Businessweek,* April 6, www.businessweek.com/ investor/content/apr2009/pi2009043_811816.htm.

[17] Boot, Arnoud W. A. (2000). "Relationship Banking: What Do We Know?" *Journal of Financial Intermediation*, vol. *9* (January), 7-25.

[18] Brevoort, Kenneth P. & Hannan, Timothy H. (2006). "Commercial Lending and Distance: Evidence from Community Reinvestment Act Data," *Journal of Money, Credit and Banking,* vol. *38* (December), 1991-2012.

[19] Bricker, Jesse, Kennickell, Arthur B., Moore, Kevin B. & John Sabelhaus (2012). "Changes in U.S. Family Finances from 2007 to 2010: Evidence from the Survey of Consumer Finances," *Federal Reserve Bulletin*, vol. *98* (June), 1-80.

[20] Cowan, Charles D. & Cowan, Adrian M. (2006). "*A Survey Based Assessment of Financial Institution Use of Credit Scoring for Small Business Lending*," unpublished paper, U.S. Small Business Administration, Office of Advocacy, November.

[21] Craig, Steven G. & Pauline Hardee (2007). "The Impact of Bank Consolidation on Small Business Credit Availability," *Journal of Banking and Finance,* vol. *31* (April), 1237-63.

[22] Critchfield, Tim, Tyler Davis, Lee Davison, Heather Gratton, George Hanc & Katherine Samolyk (2004). "The Future of Banking in America: Community Banks: Their Recent Past, Current Performance, and Future Prospects," *FDIC Banking Review,* vol. *16* (3), 1-56.

[23] Dennis, William J., Jr. (2010). *Small Business Credit in a Deep Recession.* Nashville, Tenn.: National Federation of Independent Business Research Foundation, February.

[24] —(2011). *Financing Small Businesses: Small Business and Credit Access.* Nashville, Tenn.: National Federation of Independent Business Research Foundation, January.

[25] —(2012). *Small Business, Credit Access, and a Lingering Recession.* Nashville, Tenn.: National Federation of Independent Business Research Foundation, January.

[26] DeYoung, Robert, Goldberg, Lawrence G. & White, Lawrence J. (1999). "Youth, Adolescence, and Maturity of Banks: Credit Availability to Small Business in an Era of Banking Consolidation," *Journal of Banking and Finance*, vol. *23* (February), 463-92.

[27] Group of Ten (2001). *Report on Consolidation in the Financial Sector.* Washington: International Monetary Fund, Bank for International Settlements, and Organisation for Economic Co-operation and Development, January.

[28] Jayaratne, Jith & John Wolken (1999). "How Important Are Small Banks to Small Business Lending? New Evidence from a Survey of Small Firms," *Journal of Banking and Finance*, vol. *23* (February), 427-58.

[29] Keeton, William R. (2000). "Are Mergers Responsible for the Surge in New Bank Charters?" Federal Reserve Bank of Kansas City, *Economic Review*, vol. *85* (1), 21-41.

[30] Kendall, Leon T. & Fishman, Michael J. eds. (1998). *A Primer on Securitization*. Cambridge, Mass.: MIT Press.

[31] Kiser, Elizabeth K., Prager, Robin A. & Scott, Jason R. (2012). "Supervisor Ratings and the Contraction of Bank Lending to Small Businesses," Finance and Economics Discussion Series 2012-59. Washington: Board of Governors of the Federal Reserve System.

[32] Mach, Traci L. & Wolken, John D. (2006). "Financial Services Used by Small Businesses: Evidence from the 2003 Survey of Small Business Finances," *Federal Reserve Bulletin,* vol. *92* (October), A167–A195.

[33] Mandelbaum, Robb (various years). *You're the Boss: The Art of Running a Small Business* (blog), *New York Times,* posts tagged with "A.R.C. loan," http ://boss.blogs.nytimes.com/tag/arc-loan.

[34] Moody's Investors Service (2012). "US Commercial and Esoteric ABS 2012 Outlook," *Structured Finance Special Report*, January.

[35] Ou, Charles (2005). "Banking Consolidation and Small Business Lending: A Review of Recent Research," Working Paper. Washington: U.S. Small Business Administration, Office of Advocacy, March.

[36] Peek, Joe & Rosengren, Eric S. (1998). "Bank Consolidation and Small Business Lending: It's Not Just Size That Matters," *Journal of Banking and Finance*, vol. *22* (August), 799-819.

[37] Petersen, Mitchell A. & Rajan, Raghuram G. (1995). "The Effect of Credit Market Competition on Lending Relationships," *Quarterly Journal of Economics*, vol. *110* (May), 407-43.

[38] Pilloff, Steven J. (2001). "Commercial Banking," in Walter Adams and James Brock, eds., *The Structure of American Industry*. Upper Saddle River, N.J.: Prentice-Hall.

[39] —(2004). *Bank Merger Activity in the United States, 1994 2003*, Staff Study 176. Washington: Board of Governors of the Federal Reserve System, May.

[40] Rhoades, Stephen A. (2000). *Bank Mergers and Banking Structure in the United States, 1980 98*, Staff Study 174. Washington: Board of Governors of the Federal Reserve System, August.

[41] Samolyk, Katherine & Richardson, Christopher A. (2003). "*Bank Consolidation and Small Business Lending within Local Markets*," Working Paper 03-2. Washington: Federal Deposit Insurance Corporation, April.

[42] Scott, Jonathan A., Dunkelberg, William C. & Dennis, William J. Jr. (2003). *Credit, Banks and Small Business—The New Century*. Washington: National Federation of Independent Business, January.

[43] Seelig, Steven A. & Tim Critchfield (2003). "Merger Activity as a Determinant of De Novo Entry into Urban Banking Markets," Working Paper 03-1. Washington: Federal Deposit Insurance Corporation, April.

[44] Strahan, Philip E. & Weston, James P. (1998). "Small Business Lending and the Changing Structure of the Banking Industry," *Journal of Banking and Finance*, vol. 22 (August), 821-45.

[45] U.S. Census Bureau, Population Division (2009). "Annual Population Estimates," table 1, NST-EST2009-01 (December), www.census.gov/popest/data/historical/2000s/vintage_2009/index.html.

[46] U.S. Department of Justice and Federal Trade Commission (1994). *Horizontal Merger Guidelines*. Washington: DOJ and FTC.

[47] —(2010). *Horizontal Merger Guidelines*. Washington: DOJ and FTC.

[48] U.S. Small Business Administration (2008a). "One Month LIBOR Plus 3 Percent Allowed as SBA Base Rate," SBA Procedural Notice 5000-1081 (November 14), www.sba.gov/sites/default/files/bank_5000-1081.pdf.

[49] —(2008b). "Initiative to Facilitate the Sale of SBA 7(a) Loans on the Secondary Market," SBA Procedural Notice 5000-1086 (December 17), www.sba.gov/sites/default/files/bank_5000-1086.pdf.

End Notes

[1] As required by the law, the Board consulted with the Comptroller of the Currency, the Administrator of the National Credit Union Administration, the Administrator of the Small Business Administration, the Board of Directors of the Federal Deposit Insurance Corporation, and the Secretary of Commerce.

[2] Each of the NFIB samples was drawn from the Dun & Brad-street Market Identifier File and included between 750 and 850 small employer firms. For the surveys, small employer firms were defined as firms with between 1 and 250 employees in addition to the owner(s). The samples were stratified by employment size, and weighted responses are representative of

the Dun & Bradstreet population of small employer firms in the United States in 2009, 2010, and 2011.

[3] Credit types include a renewal of an existing line of credit, a new line of credit, a new business loan, a credit card, or trade credit. In 2009, firms were also asked about their application for an equipment or vehicle loan, but this question was not asked in later years. For comparability, statistics reported here are only for firms that had an application other than an equipment or vehicle loan application in 2009.

[4] Although somewhat dated, the 2003 Survey of Small Business Finances provides the most currently available information on all sources of outstanding credit delineated by individual loans, amounts, and sources.

[5] Analysis of the small business lending activities of commercial banks and savings institutions is based on midyear Reports of Condition and Income (Call Reports) and midyear Thrift Financial Reports, which are filed by commercial banks, savings banks, and savings and loan associations. These reports include information on the number and amount of business loans outstanding with original amounts of $1 million or less.

[6] The outstanding business loans from credit unions are not directly comparable with those of commercial banks because the credit union Call Reports do not allow construction and land development and agricultural loans to be taken out of the total.

[7] For example, see Dennis (2011) and Dennis (2012).

[8] For an analysis of the 2007 09 financial crisis, see Bernanke (2010).

[9] Data used in this section are from the flow of funds accounts published by the Federal Reserve Board, Consolidated Reports of Condition and Income for banks, and surveys of lenders and of small businesses. Information from the flow of funds accounts relates to organizational type rather than to size of firm. A business can be organized as a corporation (C type or S type), a proprietorship, or a partnership. Most proprietorships and partnerships are small businesses. Large, publicly traded firms are generally C corporations, which are subject to corporate income taxes and securities laws. The S type of corporation is designed primarily for small businesses and generally is not subject to corporate income taxes.

[10] In this section, data on partnerships and proprietorships are from the flow of funds accounts published by the Federal Reserve Board, and total small business debt is approximated by unincorporated nonfinancial business debt from the flow of funds accounts. These data may include some large proprietorships and partnerships, which would not be considered small businesses.

[11] Each month, the NFIB polls a random sample of its members to assess business conditions and the availability of credit for small businesses. For the first month of each quarter, roughly 11,000 firms receive questionnaires, and about 2,000 typically respond; for the remaining two months of each quarter, about 4,000 questionnaires are mailed, with around 800 responses. About 90 percent of the respondents have fewer than 40 employees.

[12] The SLOOS is available on the Federal Reserve Board's website at www.federalreserve.gov/boarddocs/SnLoanSurvey.

[13] Data on small business loan prices (interest rates and fees) are not publicly reported or widely available. Therefore, the analysis and discussion of pricing in this chapter are limited.

[14] County Business Patterns data are compiled from the Business Register, a database of all known single and multi-establishment employer companies maintained and updated by the Census Bureau. The data cover most industries, excluding crop and animal production; rail transportation; national postal service; pension, health, welfare, and vacation funds; trusts, estates, and agency accounts; private households; and public administration. The data also exclude most establishments reporting government employees. For more details on the data, see U.S. Census Bureau, "County Business Patterns: About the Data," webpage, www.census.gov/econ/cbp/overview.htm.

[15] The data set excludes data on self-employed individuals, employees of private households, railroad employees, agricultural production employees, and most government employees. Businesses operating without an employer identification number (EIN), and businesses with

an EIN but without employees, are also excluded from the County Business Patterns universe.

[16] The data in the figure are specific to establishments that first reported having employees in 1994. The trends are similar for establishments born in later years. The 1994 cohort is used because it has the longest history available.

[17] Banks typically provide multiple products to small businesses that borrow from them. The 2003 Survey of Small Business Finances indicates that small firms that obtained at least one product at a commercial bank averaged 2.1 products at that bank. The comparable average number of products at nonbanks was 1.3. Small firms with at least one product at a bank had one or more other products at that bank almost 60 percent of the time. In contrast, more than 80 percent of small firms that had a product with a nonbank provider obtained no other products from the nonbank.

[18] A detailed description of the process of relationship lending and the way it differs from nonrelationship lending is provided by Berger and Udell (2002). Boot (2000) and Berger and Udell (1998) include detailed discussions of the costs and benefits of relationship lending, including a review of the literature.

[19] Recent information on community banks and relationship lending is in Critchfield and others (2004) and Avery and Samolyk (2004).

[20] Bank Call Reports do not provide information on delinquency rates by size of borrower or size of loan. We look at delinquency rates on all C&I loans and all CRE loans at banks that have a high concentration of small loans to businesses as proxies for performance on small C&I and small CRE loans.

[21] For more information on the 2009, 2010, and 2011 surveys, see Dennis (2010), Dennis (2011), and Dennis (2012), respectively.

[22] Each of the surveys was conducted in the fourth quarter of the year, so the reference period was the first three quarters of the survey year and the last quarter of the prior year. For ease of exposition, this chapter will refer to the period with the year of the survey. Figures reported in this chapter are calculated from the microdata provided by the NFIB.

[23] A portion of the differences in patterns observed across the three years of data may be attributable to sampling variability.

[24] Data from the 1998 and 2003 Surveys of Small Business Finances indicate that in 1998, 76 percent of small businesses that used either business or personal credit cards paid off their balances each month; in 2003, this figure was 70.7 percent. For more information, see Mach and Wolken (2006) and Bitler, Robb, and Wolken (2001).

[25] Detailed usage information is not available for 2009 due to an error in the questionnaire pattern that caused cell sizes to be very small and detailed statistics to be unreliable.

[26] Data from the 1998 and 2003 Surveys of Small Business Finances indicate that in 1998, 34.1 percent of small businesses used business credit cards; by 2003, this figure had increased to 48.1 percent. During the same period, the use of personal credit cards increased less than 1 percentage point.

[27] Although the NFIB surveys did collect information on outcomes for credit card applications, they asked only about the most recent application, regardless of whether the application was personal or business. This approach leaves only a small number of observations for each type of credit card application and even fewer observations when broken down by size. Such comparisons are unreliable.

[28] This fraction of firms is very similar to that reported using trade credit in the 1998 and 2003 Surveys of Small Business Finances.

[29] Credit types include a renewal of an existing line of credit, a new line of credit, a new business loan, a credit card, or trade credit. In 2009, firms were also asked about their application for an equipment or vehicle loan, but this question was not asked in later years. For

comparability, statistics reported here are only for firms that had an application other than an equipment or vehicle loan application in 2009.

[30] This low denial rate for the smallest firms is likely related to the relationship between the age and size of the firm. While most young firms are small, not all small firms are young. The older a firm is, the more information is likely to be available for credit decisions to be based on.

[31] We lack sufficient information to determine the extent to which the decline in PAYDEX scores among survey respondents reflects sample variability from one year to the next as opposed to a change in the distribution of credit scores for the population of small businesses.

[32] The question asked was, "In the last 12 months, was there credit the firm wanted, but did not apply for, because management didn't think you could get it?"

[33] The 1998 and 2003 Surveys of Small Business Finances asked a similar question, using the past three years, rather than just the previous year, as the reference period. Only 18 percent of firms in 2003, and 23 percent of firms in 1998, reported this experience. In addition, the longer reference period would tend to lead to more instances in which firms may have forgone applying for credit, biasing the results of the three-year question higher. The fact that the three-year figure is lower in absolute terms than the one-year figure observed recently would tend to indicate higher levels of discouraged borrowers in the current period.

[34] Savings institutions (or thrifts) consist of savings banks and savings and loan associations.

[35] Although somewhat dated, the 2003 SSBF provides the most currently available information on all sources of outstanding credit delineated by individual loans, amounts, and sources.

[36] The majority of other loans were loans that could not be classified as credit lines, mortgages, vehicle loans, equipment loans, or capital leases. Such loans were most likely term (loans that typically carry a fixed interest rate and a fixed maturity, generally repaid in monthly installations) or signature loans (fixed-term unsecured loans secured by a personal signature and promise to repay), and roughly 70 percent were unsecured.

[37] The 2010 SCF was expanded to elicit additional information from households that owned small businesses with fewer than 500 employees. For more information on the survey, see Bricker and others (2012). "Primary" was determined by the respondent. The percentage reported is based on households with a small business that reported using a financial institution for their business.

[38] For more information on the NFIB yearly surveys in 2009, 2010, and 2011, see the "Credit Use by Small Businesses" section earlier in this chapter.

[39] Another source of data on small business loans is the information reported pursuant to the regulations (such as the Federal Reserve Board's Regulation BB) that implement the Community Reinvestment Act (CRA). The data collected include information on credit extensions for small businesses, small farms, and community development. The data are not analyzed in this chapter because the regulations that implement the CRA were modified in 2005 to eliminate mandated reporting for institutions with assets less than $1 billion. As a result, the number of institutions providing data has fallen sharply. In 2006, only about 1,000 banks and thrifts, or 11 percent of the total, reported data. For CRA reporters, the CRA data on loan originations is highly correlated with the June Call Report data on outstanding loans. However, most CRA reporters are very large institutions, which may differ significantly from smaller ones. More information on CRA-related small business lending is available on the Federal Financial Institutions Examination Council's website at www.ffiec.gov/cra/default.htm.

[40] Analysis in this section is based on Call Report and TFR data from June 2011.

[41] For loans drawn down under lines of credit or loan commitments, the original amount of the loan is the size of the line of credit or loan commitment when it was most recently approved, extended, or renewed before the report date. If the amount currently outstanding

exceeds this size, the original amount is the amount currently outstanding as of the report date. For loan participations and syndications, the original amount is the entire amount of the credit originated by the lead lender. For all other loans, the original amount is the total amount of the loan at origination or the amount currently outstanding as of the report date, whichever is larger.

[42] Other unreported small business loans include home mortgage and other consumer loans that are used by small business owners for commercial purposes. Data from the 2010 SCF indicate that 16 percent of business owners report using personal assets to guarantee or collateralize loans for their businesses and 14 percent report lending money directly to the business. Such loans are not in statistics from the Call Reports or TFRs.

[43] According to the 2003 SSBF, the median line of credit commitment was $50,000. In contrast, the 3.5 percent of commitments that were larger than $1 million had a median of $3.3 million.

[44] Except where indicated, bank data are aggregated to the banking organization level by summing data for all commonly owned commercial banking institutions. The organization is considered a single entity. Data for affiliated nonbank subsidiaries are excluded.

[45] A thorough discussion of merger activity in the banking industry is in Adams (2012), Avery and Samolyk (2004), Group of Ten (2001), Pilloff (2001, 2004), Rhoades (2000), or Berger, Demsetz, and Strahan (1999).

[46] Data on bank mergers and acquisitions between 2000 and 2010 are from Adams (2012). Data for the years 1999 and 2011 were updated with information from Call Reports, Summary of Deposit statistics, and data from SNL Financial. Dollar lending to small business is available in table 1.

[47] With Call Report and TFR data, business loans of $1 million or less are considered small.

[48] A general review is in Ou (2005). Studies have typically focused on small business credit supplied by commercial banks. Credit obtained from other financial or nonfinancial firms has usually not been included in the analyses. Such studies provide a somewhat incomplete picture of small business lending, but because banks are the primary supplier of credit to small businesses, findings based on bank lending are likely to be relevant to the overall provision of small business credit.

[49] Data from the 2003 SSBF indicate that between 1998 and 2003, the share of credit obtained by small businesses from nonbank financial institutions increased from 27 percent to 35 percent. During the same period, the share of credit obtained by small businesses from commercial banks fell from 65 percent to 57 percent. Nonbank financial institutions include thrifts, credit unions, and finance, insurance, leasing, and mortgage companies. Related data are in table A.5 of Board of Governors (2007) and table A.5 of Board of Governors (2002).

[50] Other sources showing the importance of proximity for small business lenders are CRA data and surveys conducted by the NFIB. The CRA data indicate that the vast majority of small business loan originations are made by in-market lenders (Board of Governors, 2002, p. 46). Brevoort and Hannan (2006, p. 4), using CRA data, report that distance is negatively associated with the probability of a small business loan being made and that "there has been no discernible increase in the distance between lenders and their local borrowers . . . in recent years." NFIB surveys indicate that the majority of small business financial institutions are located within 10 minutes of borrowers' offices (Scott, Dunkelberg, and Dennis, 2003).

[51] A thorough summary of the literature on relationship lending is in Boot (2000) and Berger and Udell (1998).

[52] In assessing the likely competitive effects of proposed bank mergers and acquisitions, both the Federal Reserve Board and the Department of Justice use local deposits as a proxy for a banking organization's capacity to provide a cluster of commercial banking products and services within a banking market.

[53] In reviewing bank merger applications, the Federal Reserve Board typically computes HHIs that give commercial bank deposits a weight of 100 percent and thrift deposits a weight of

50 percent. This "downweighting" of thrifts reflects the fact that they are generally less active in commercial lending than are commercial banks and hence should not be considered "full competitors" in the provision of banking services. On a case-by-case basis, the deposits of those thrifts that are active commercial lenders are given a weight of 100 percent in the Federal Reserve Board's calculations.

[54] A value of 10000 indicates perfect monopoly, and zero indicates perfect competition. Under the 1994 *Horizontal Merger Guidelines* of the U.S. Department of Justice and the Federal Trade Commission, a market in which the HHI is less than 1000 is considered unconcentrated, one in which it ranges from 1000 to 1800 is considered moderately concentrated, and one in which it is greater than 1800 is considered highly concentrated (see U.S. Department of Justice and Federal Trade Commission, 1994). The *Horizontal Merger Guidelines* were updated in 2010. Under the 2010 guidelines, a market in which the HHI is less than 1500 is considered unconcentrated, one in which it ranges from 1500 to 2500 is considered moderately concentrated, and one in which it is greater than 2500 is considered highly concentrated (see U.S. Department of Justice and Federal Trade Commission, 2010). In the commercial banking industry, antitrust enforcement still relies on the 1994 guidelines.

[55] Kiser, Prager, and Scott (2012) find that the distribution of banks' supervisory ratings shifted toward worse ratings between 2007 and 2010, and that those ratings downgrades were associated with significantly lower rates of growth in small business lending over this period.

[56] Savings institutions also make loans to businesses. Unlike commercial banks, federal savings institutions have statutory restrictions on the type of lending they may do; in the case of business lending, they may hold no more than 20 percent of their assets in commercial loans, and any amounts in excess of 10 percent must be used only for small business loans.

[57] The 2003 SSBF data corroborate these findings. Thrifts accounted for about 6 percent of total outstanding small business loans, whereas banks accounted for 56.8 percent. Nearly three-fourths of the small business dollars outstanding at thrifts were mortgage loans. In contrast, almost one-half of such dollars outstanding at commercial banks were lines of credit.

[58] The outstanding business loans from credit unions are not directly comparable with those of commercial banks because the credit union Call Reports do not allow construction and land development and agricultural loans to be taken out of the total.

[59] See H.R. 3380, Promoting Lending to America's Small Businesses Act of 2009, and S. 2919, Small Business Lending Enhancement Act of 2009, for more information.

[60] In the 1998 SSBF, 69.1 percent of dollars outstanding were owed to depository institutions, and 13.4 percent were owed to finance companies; in 2003, 63.7 percent of dollars outstanding were owed to depository institutions, and 16.2 percent were owed to finance companies.

[61] According to data from the G.20 Statistical Release, "Finance Companies," loans and leases for motor vehicles and business equipment accounted for 70 to 80 percent of all outstanding business loans between 2007 and February 2012. The G.20 Statistical Release is available on the Federal Reserve Board's web-site at www.federalreserve.gov/releases/g20/current/g20.htm.

[62] The result of the 2008 SEC regulation is most apparent for Prosper.com, which had been responsible for nearly 80 percent of total dollar volume prior to the shutdown (see Bogoslaw, 2009).

[63] No information is provided on the size of the firms borrowing funds; however, given the small size of the loans, it is inferred that all peer-to-peer lending to businesses is to small businesses.

[64] For census tracts in an MSA, the MSA would be considered the broader area. For census tracts outside of an MSA, all non-MSA counties within the same state would be considered the broader area.

[65] For credit cards and lines of credit in the CRA data, banks report new and renewed line sizes (the maximum amount of available credit) as the amount originated. More details on CRA reporting requirements and standards are available on the Federal Financial Institutions Examination Council's website at www.ffiec.gov/cra/default.htm.

[66] One example is FIA Card Services, which is a subsidiary of Bank of America Corporation and specializes in credit card issuance for the Bank of America organization.

[67] It is important to keep in mind that the CRA data exclude a large number of smaller banks that may account for a significant number of loans, and therefore the share of lending attributed to the top 10 organizations is overstated in the CRA data.

[68] As a special provision of the American Recovery and Reinvestment Act of 2009, guarantees were temporarily increased.

[69] More information on implementing ARRA is available on the SBA's website at http://archive.sba.gov/recovery/REC_ LEARN_PROGRAMS.html.

[70] Additional details are in Mandelbaum (various years).

[71] More information on the Small Business Jobs Act is available on the SBA's website at www.sba.gov/content/small-business-jobs-act-2010.

[72] For more details on the Small Business Lending Fund, see the Treasury Department's website, www.treasury.gov/resource-center/sb-programs/Pages/Small-Business-Lending-Fund.aspx.

[73] More information on traditional and nontraditional financing sources can be found earlier in this chapter in the section "Providers of Credit to Small Businesses."

[74] As previously mentioned, Call Reports do not provide information on loans by the size of the firm but rather by the size of the initial loan; loans with original values of less than $1 million are used as a proxy for small business lending. Information by the original size of the loan was available only yearly until 2010, at which time it became available every quarter.

[75] Although credit scoring has the potential to increase the uniformity of underwriting procedures and standards for small business loans, thereby expanding access to secondary markets, Cowan and Cowan (2006, p. viii) report that "there is no indication of any momentum in the development of secondary markets for small business loans." Their survey finds that respondents generally did not view secondary-market sales as an important reason for adopting small business credit scoring.

[76] For more information on the TALF, see the Federal Reserve Board's website at www.federalreserve.gov/newsevents/reform_ talf.htm.

[77] For more information on Moody's forecast, see Moody's Investors Service (2012).

[78] For example, see Dennis (2011) and Dennis (2012).

In: Small Business Lending
Editor: Barbara Schwartz
ISBN: 978-1-62417-480-3

Chapter 2

SMALL BUSINESS CREDIT AVAILABILITY*

Elizabeth A. Duke

It's a pleasure to be here this morning. I appreciate the opportunity to take part in this conference and to talk with you about credit conditions--especially conditions in the small business lending market. Credit availability is a necessary component of economic recovery, and factoring represents an important source of credit for large and small businesses.

Credit markets normally recover slowly following financial crises, and the most recent episode was no exception. However, after declining throughout 2009 and much of 2010, recent measures of aggregate credit outstanding have shown some signs of improvement. Nonrevolving consumer credit outstanding, which includes auto and student lending, has increased for the past seven months. Issuance of corporate bonds has been robust for several quarters, and new issuance of commercial mortgage-backed securities picked up in the first quarter of 2011, albeit from very low levels. Commercial and industrial (C&I) loans outstanding have resumed growing modestly on average.

While credit availability seemed to improve for large companies throughout the past year, small businesses still complained of difficulty in

* This is an edited, reformatted and augmented version of remarks made by the Board of Governors of the Federal Reserve System at the 2011 Factoring Conference, dated April 14, 2011.

gaining access to credit. Recent anecdotes lead me to believe that conditions are improving for small businesses, but data are scarce for this market. Today I will pull together information from a variety of sources, including surveys of small businesses and surveys of lenders, to paint a picture of the credit conditions currently facing small businesses.

SOURCES OF FINANCING FOR NEW AND EXISTING SMALL BUSINESSES

Small businesses are central to creating jobs and to restoring our economic prosperity. The economic importance of small businesses is due in part to the fact that about one-half of all Americans are employed by firms with fewer than 500 employees. In addition, business start-ups are a critical component of the experimentation process that contributes to restructuring and growth in the United States on an ongoing basis. Indeed, each wave of firm start-ups creates a substantial number of jobs. Over the past two decades, firms less than two years old accounted for about one-fourth of gross job creation even though such enterprises employed less than 10 percent of the workforce.[1] But, as a note of caution, these young firms also have high job destruction rates; within five years of starting up, about 40 percent of the jobs initially created have been eliminated by the firms' exit from their market. The "up or out" dynamics of start-ups and young firms are consistent with the innovation, learning, and market selection that is associated with entrepreneurship.

Given the key role that start-up and established small businesses play in job creation, it is useful to consider how start-ups are typically funded and how the owners of more-mature, but still small, businesses tend to support their ongoing operations. To this end, the Federal Reserve's 2010 Survey of Consumer Finances (SCF) provides some new and very preliminary data regarding the primary sources of money used to start, acquire, or expand closely held businesses.[2] The survey was conducted largely over the second half of 2010.

In this discussion, I will focus on the responses by owners of businesses with fewer than 500 employees that were in operation at the time of our survey. For these small and nascent businesses, more than 70 percent were initiated using personal savings or assets, about 6 percent were initiated using a personal loan from a bank or savings institution, about 3 percent were initiated using a personal or business credit card, and just 3 percent were initiated using a business loan from a bank or savings institution. Even smaller percentages of start-up small businesses appear to have received funding from credit unions, other institutions, or investors. In short, our survey data suggest that the personal resources of entrepreneurs are the most important funding source for small business formation.

The importance of personal resources in financing small businesses is supported by other recent survey evidence. In our 2009 panel SCF, we found that families make loan guarantees for their businesses using personal assets as collateral, and that loans between business owners and their businesses are common in both directions.[3] Moreover, according to the most recently available data from the U.S. Census Bureau's Survey of Business Owners, 6 in 10 small business owners use personal savings or assets to finance or expand their businesses.

These responses highlight the role personal wealth plays in business formation. Looking back at wealth outcomes in 2009, we found that 43 percent of families saw a wealth decline equal to or greater than six months of their usual income, and almost one-third saw a loss greater than an entire year of the usual income.[4] Such wealth declines would, of course, reduce the likelihood that such households would start a small business.

Over the same period, however, about one-fifth of families saw a gain in wealth that was greater than six months of their usual income. Moreover, a higher percentage of business owners who participated in the survey saw larger wealth gains relative to their incomes than was the case for the overall population. These findings suggest that there just might be a pool of potential entrepreneurs who have both the resources and relevant experience to start successful businesses.

Turning to the funding needs of more-mature businesses, in the 2010 SCF, we asked small business owners whether and to what extent external sources of money were used to finance the ongoing operations of or improvements to their primary businesses in the past year. Focusing again on only businesses with fewer than 500 employees, the preliminary survey data suggest that for such purposes, slightly less than one-half of these businesses did not use any external funding. Consistent with the funding information on the start-up phase for small businesses, a significant proportion of small business owners--about one-third--used their personal savings or assets to fund operations or make improvements. And only small percentages of small business owners obtained credit from a bank or savings institution for such purposes: Among these small business owners, about 5 percent used personal or business credit cards, slightly less than 5 percent used business loans, and about 3 percent used personal loans.

Taken together, these survey data suggest that many small business owners do not tap the credit markets, but instead use their own wherewithal to start and fund their businesses. Indeed, a bit less than 80 percent of small business owner survey respondents with fewer than 500 employees indicated that they had not even applied for business loans in the past five years. This is not to say that loans are not important--far from it-but that for a broad range of businesses, personal finances may be the determining factor in starting a business, and personal finances may also be most important in sustaining the health of a business once started.

So what happened to the small business owners who did apply for loans? The turndown rate was fairly modest--about 12 percent. Moreover, for those small business owners who received credit, more than 90 percent of those surveyed actually received as much credit as they had requested. These results are perhaps surprising given that two of the past five years were ones with very tight credit conditions by historical standards, and anecdotal evidence suggests that many lines of credit, for businesses and for households, were cut during the recent financial crisis.

Furthermore, small business lending is an important part of overall bank lending, especially at community banks. According to regulatory data, small loans to businesses, a proxy for loans to small businesses, constituted 23 percent of total business loans outstanding at commercial banks at the end of 2010.[5] Over the past several years, this share has fluctuated between 22 and 27 percent of banks' business lending. In addition, at community banks with less than $1 billion in assets, the share is higher--around 66 percent--whereas at larger banks with more than $10 billion in assets, the share is lower--16 percent.

SMALL BUSINESS CONCERNS

The foregoing survey data on turndown rates and credit constraints for small business owners are consistent with other survey evidence collected by the National Federation of Independent Business (NFIB). In fact, over the past five years, small business owners identified weak demand, taxes, and government regulations more frequently than interest rates and credit conditions as their most important problem. During that period, less than 5 percent of small business respondents typically identified interest rates and credit conditions as their most important problem. In contrast, 25 percent or more of small business owners considered weak demand the most important concern during much of the past three-year period (figure 1). In considering responses to this question, however, it is important to remember that the survey allows owners to identify only their most important problem, not a set of problems. It is possible that financing was the second-most-important problem, but we would not know it from this set of data.

Even if tight credit is not the most important concern, perceptions of tight credit still might significantly influence the decisions made by current and prospective small business owners. Among the small business borrowers surveyed by the NFIB, a fairly high net percentage--about 8 percent in March--continues to report that credit is more difficult to obtain than it was three months ago (figure 2). This level of self-reported perceptions of tighter credit for small businesses is about the same as was observed in 2007--a period prior to the recent business cycle peak. It is also well below the 16 percent of small business respondents, on net, who perceived that credit had become more difficult to obtain in 2009.

Looking back to 2009, a Ewing Marion Kauffman Foundation longitudinal study of small businesses that were founded in 2004 and tracked since then found that 89 percent of the surviving firms that were denied loans in that year felt that banks' heightened requirements played a role in their denials.[6] Among the small businesses that were tracked, 21 percent had chosen not to apply for loans for fear of being denied credit, and 5 percent also refrained from seeking external equity financing for fear of being denied such financing. So it seems that perceptions of credit tightness may lead some small business owners to decide not even to try to obtain additional funding.

At this time, however, the net percentage of survey respondents telling the NFIB that they expect credit conditions to become tighter over the next three months has come down considerably from what small business owners reported during 2009. This decrease suggests that, compared with the previous few years, far fewer small business owners are expecting that credit conditions will remain tight.

Overall, what seems to matter most with regard to funding, from the small business owner's viewpoint, is one's personal savings or assets, the internally generated funds derived from operating the business, expected sales, and the fact that credit conditions seem to be less tight, so money is available, if and when it is needed.

(Monthly data, 1986-2011)

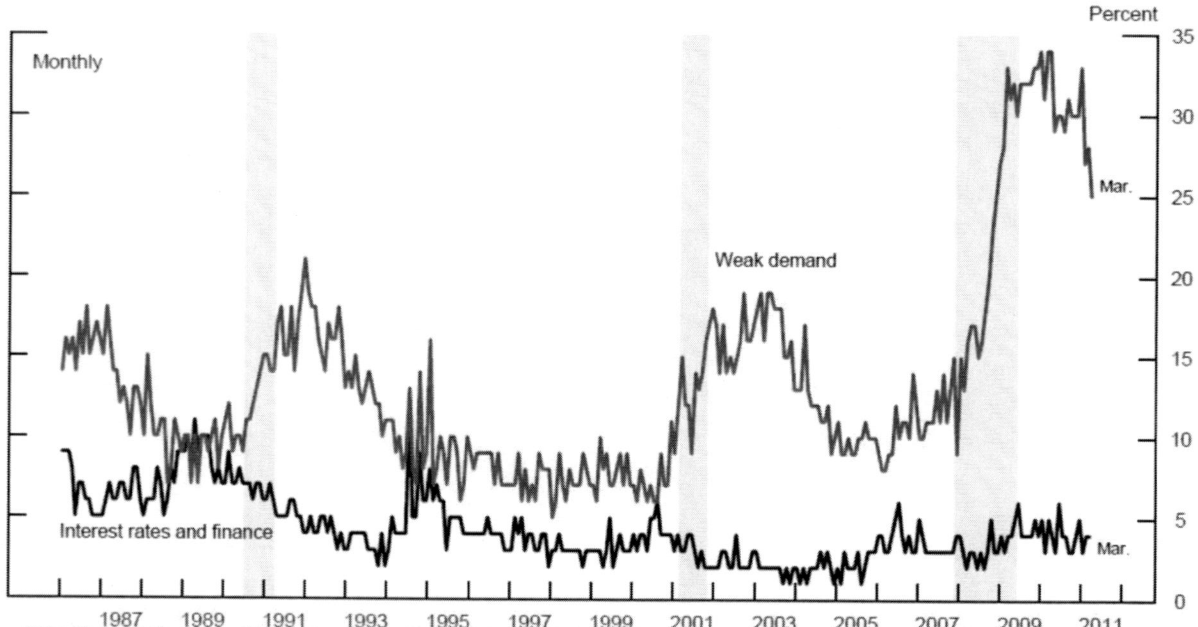

Note: Respondents can report that their most important problem is: weak demand, interest rates and finance, inflation, taxes, government regulation, cost and availability of insurance, quality of labor, cost of labor, competition from large businesses, and other. Not seasonally adjusted. Shaded areas denote National Bureau of Economic Research recession periods.

Source: National Federation of Independent Business (NFIB).

Figure 1. NFIB survey results on most important problem for small businesses (selected categories).

(Monthly data, 1990-2011)

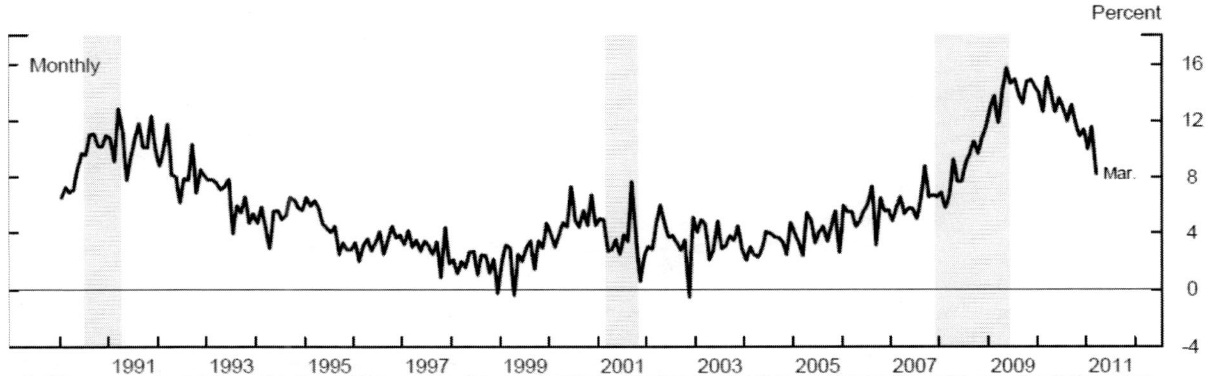

* Of borrowers who sought credit in the past three months, the proportion that reported more difficulty in obtaining credit less the proportion that reported more ease in obtaining credit. Seasonally adjusted by the Federal Reserve Board. Shaded areas denote National Bureau of Economic Research recession periods.

Source: National Federation of Independent Business (NFIB).

Figure 2. Credit more difficult to obtain than 3 months ago (net)*.

Business Conditions for Small Businesses

Currently, expectations about future sales seem to be more important than expectations about the availability of credit in driving business spending decisions and demand for business loans. Recently, small business owners appear to have become more optimistic about their outlook for sales. For example, in recent NFIB surveys, the net percentage of respondents who expected their sales to increase rose to levels not seen since mid-2007 (figure 3).

More generally, small business owners surveyed by the NFIB indicate that they currently expect business conditions to improve in the near future. In fact, the net percentage of small business respondents who expected business conditions to improve six months from now climbed in February to its highest level in several years (figure 4). Even with some backtracking in March, this barometer of business conditions remains at a level not seen since mid-2007.

Other survey data collected by the NFIB are also consistent with more-favorable conditions for small businesses. The percentages of small business respondents who believe it is a good time to expand, and who plan to make capital expenditures over the next three to six months, have recently risen to levels not seen since mid-2007.

The Bankers' Perspective on Lending to Small Businesses

Mirroring small business respondents views with respect to credit conditions are bankers' views on credit standards and their terms of credit. To consider the bankers' perspective, I will draw on two other Federal Reserve surveys: the Senior Loan Officer Opinion Survey on Bank Lending Practices (SLOOS) and the Survey of Terms of Business Lending (STBL). With regard to credit standards, we found that about 5 percent of banks, on net, reported in January that they had eased their bank's lending standards on commercial and industrial loans to small firms in the fourth quarter of last year (figure 5).[7] A similar net fraction of banks reported having eased standards in the previous survey. This finding is consistent with small business owners' perceptions that credit conditions have eased somewhat.

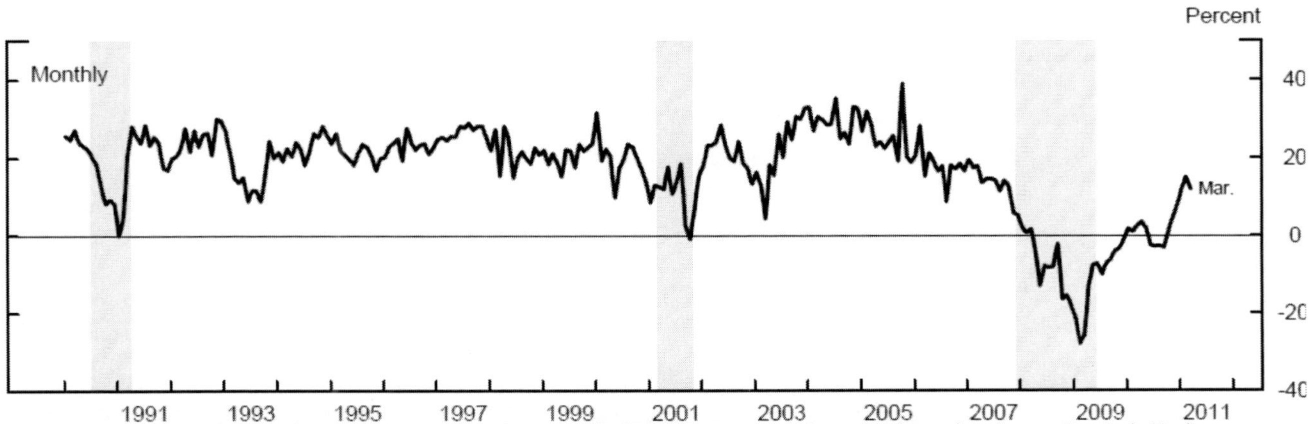

* Net percent of respondents that expect higher sales less the percent that expect lower sales in the next three months. Seasonally adjusted by the Federal Reserve Board. Shaded areas denote National Bureau of Economic Research recession periods.

Source: National Federation of Independent Business (NFIB).

Figure 3. Sales expected to increase over next 3 months (net)*.

(Monthly data, 1990-2011)

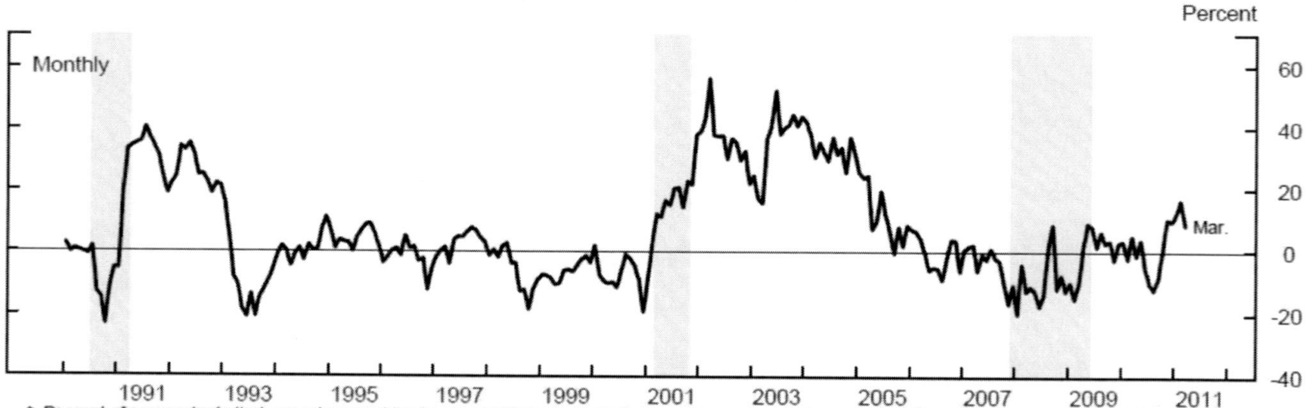

* Percent of respondents that expect general business conditions to be better less the percent that expect conditions to be worse. Seasonally adjusted by the Federal Reserve Board. Shaded areas denote National Bureau of Economic Research recession periods.

Source: National Federation of Independent Business (NFIB).

Figure 4. Outlook for general business conditions 6 months from now (net)*.

(Quarterly data, 1990-2011)

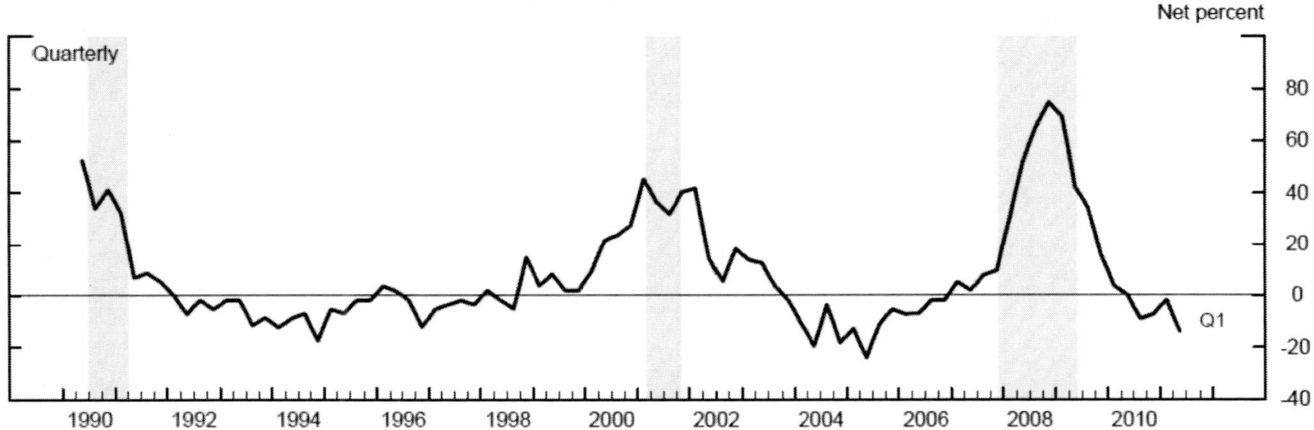

Note: Shaded areas denote National Bureau of Economic Research recession periods.
Source: Senior Loan Officer Opinion Survey on Bank Lending Practices, Federal Reserve Board.

Figure 5. Change in standards for commercial and industrial loans to small firms.

For those small business owners whose loans or credit lines were approved, the terms of credit--the interest rate spread over the bank's cost of funds, the cost of a credit line, the maturity, and the size of a loan--are practical measures that can be used to assess credit availability. The January SLOOS indicates that about one-third of banks, on net, reported that they had trimmed the spreads of C&I loan rates over their costs of funds on loans to small firms (figure 6). Somewhat smaller net fractions of these loan officers reported that they had lowered the costs of credit lines and lengthened the maximum maturities of loans to small firms. Despite the fact that such terms of credit were eased for small firms, the banks reported that the maximum sizes of C&I loans, and limits on credit lines and business credit card accounts, remained unchanged over the past two surveys. This result means that such lines were not being cut as they were during the first half of 2010. Easing of credit conditions usually does not occur until banks see improvement in the credit metrics of existing portfolios. In the January SLOOS, 77 percent of bankers reported having seen an improvement in the quality of existing loans to small firms.

The SLOOS does not distinguish between commercial real estate loans to small firms and such loans to others, but we know that real-estate-secured lending is an important source of credit for small businesses. The respondents to the January SLOOS indicated that there was little movement, on net, in domestic banks' lending standards for commercial real estate loans over the past two surveys (figure 7). Such standards remain relatively tight even though more than one-half of banks expect an improvement in the quality of commercial real estate loans. And, importantly for small business owners, the commercial bank Call Reports indicated that as of the end of last year, the loans secured by owner-occupied property had continued to outperform other commercial real estate loans.

Information contained in the February STBL also indicated a recent easing of terms on bank loans. More specifically, recent loan rate spreads on C&I loans at domestic banks were lower, on average, regardless of the bank's size, and the average number of days to maturity had lengthened.

The recent easing in banks' lending policies and banks' improved expectations with respect to credit quality are indications that financing conditions for at least some small businesses are likely improving.

(Quarterly data, 1990-2011)

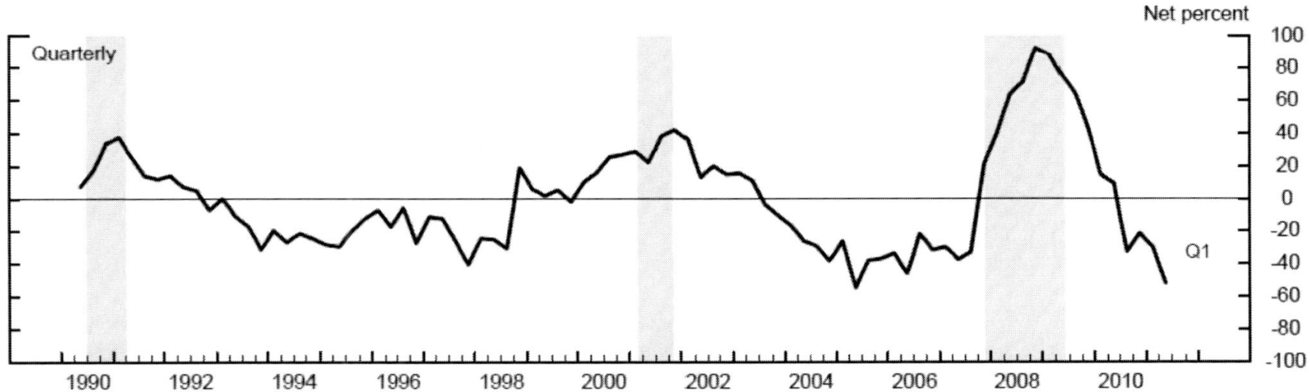

Tight = Wider spreads
Note: Shaded areas denote National Bureau of Economic Research recession periods.
Source: Senior Loan Officer Opinion Survey on Bank Lending Practices, Federal Reserve Board.

Figure 6. Change in spreads of loan rates over cost of funds to small firms.

(Quarterly data, 1990-2011)

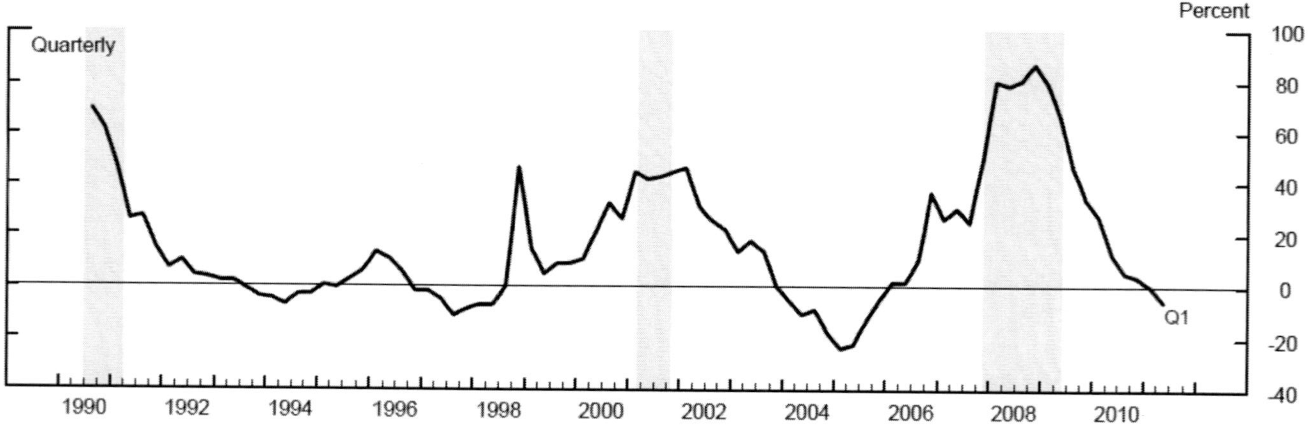

Note: Shaded areas denote National Bureau of Economic Research recession periods.
Source: Senior Loan Officer Opinion Survey on Bank Lending Practices, Federal Reserve Board.

Figure 7. Change in standards for commercial real estate loans.

By and large, small business owners' perceptions about the tightness of credit conditions seem to be aligned fairly well with bankers' perceptions of late. Such perceptions are also consistent with recent turndown statistics. According to the National Small Business Association (NSBA), the percentage of small business owners reporting an inability to obtain adequate financing declined to 36 percent at year-end from 41 percent in July 2010.[8] These data, of course, apply to members of the NSBA, whereas the SCF data I discussed earlier apply in principle to all small business owners, even owners of quite small businesses who might be unlikely to join an association. This may explain the much higher credit use among NSBA members.

LENDING TO SMALL BUSINESSES

So far, I have discussed measures of business credit. But, as I noted earlier, small businesses also rely on personal accounts and loans, household credit cards, trade credit from other nonfinancial firms, and other sources, including factoring. The effect of these other sources of funding on businesses' finances is even more difficult to determine from available data.

Changes in personal wealth during the downturn were not uniform across households, and there were some big winners and losers. While the households that disproportionately increased their wealth are more likely to start businesses, those that disproportionately lost wealth are less likely to do so. In particular, the recent housing downturn has made it more difficult to use cash-out refinancing or home equity lending as a funding vehicle for small business formation. It has also made it more difficult for some small business owners to fund the purchase of equipment or to cover business operating expenses.

Even though our survey data suggest that only 3 to 5 percent of small business owners tend to rely on personal or business credit cards, the decline in bank credit card outstandings over most of the past two years indicates that this source of credit may still be quite limited.

While balance sheet data for financial institutions are readily available, the relative contributions to changes in outstanding balances of new lending, paydowns, and write-downs and the levels of line usage are not available. To focus on the link between lending and new business activity, we need measures of loan originations. Indeed, a loan or lease origination is what typically generates an investment in equipment and signals business growth.[9]

To explore recent loan and lease originations to small businesses, we can look at the PayNet/Thomson Reuters Small Business Lending Index (SBLI).

For inclusion in this index, a loan or lease must be originated to a business borrower who has total loan outstandings across all qualifying lenders of less than $1 million at both the start and the end of the month in question. While some such loans and leases may be to established firms that employ more than 500 workers, small businesses are generally viewed as much more likely to borrow in these relatively small loan denominations. The lenders that provide the data used to construct the index are banks and finance companies.

The year-over-year changes in the SBLI are consistent with a view that loan originations are a pro-cyclical indicator (figure 8). Strikingly, such year-over-year changes were mainly positive, but smaller through time, until the recent business cycle peak in December 2007. During the recession, however, the year-over-year changes in the SBLI were increasingly negative until the business cycle trough, which occurred in June 2009. Then, shortly after the recent business cycle trough, the year-over-year negative changes in the index became smaller until they turned positive in early 2010. In February, the most recent month for which data are available, the SBLI measure of business loan and lease originations rose 15 percent from a year earlier.

The seasonally adjusted index, which is normalized to 100 in January 2005, provides a different take on small business originations (figure 9). This measure of lending, which allows comparisons across different months, has not yet rebounded to its level in mid-2007 even though many of the measures of small business owners' and bankers' perspectives have returned to their pre-recession levels. Despite the magnitude of the rebound, there has been an apparent turnaround in loan and lease originations using the seasonally adjusted SBLI measure. These data add to the evidence that credit availability to small businesses is gradually improving.

While at first glance stronger demand for bank loans by large and medium-sized firms may seem irrelevant for analyzing credit to small businesses, that perception would ignore the fact that such demand may signal that larger firms are becoming more willing to provide trade credit to smaller firms that are their suppliers or customers. In the most recent SLOOS, the net percentage of respondents reporting higher loan demand by large and medium-sized firms rose above 20 percent for the first time since 2005 (figure 10). That said, banks report that loan demand from smaller firms remains fairly weak. Only a small net percentage of banks reported stronger demand from such firms.

(Monthly data, 2006-11)

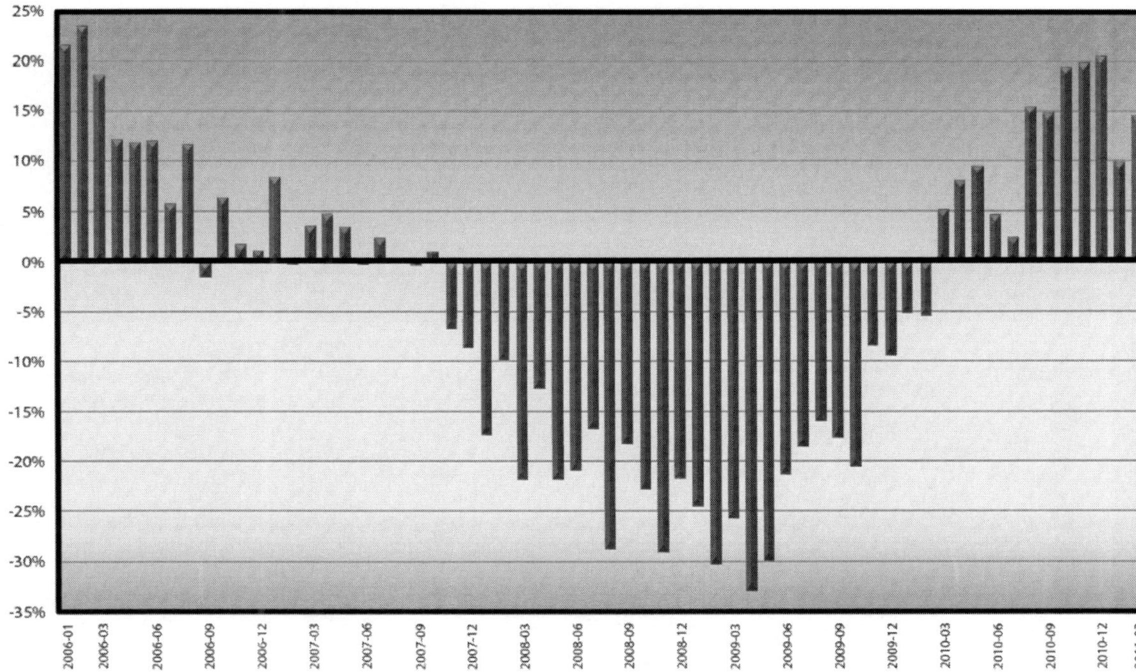

SBLI Small Business Lending Index.
Source: PayNet/Thomson Reuters.

Figure 8. PayNet/Thomson Reuters SBLI percent change vs. year prior.

(Monthly data, 2005-11)

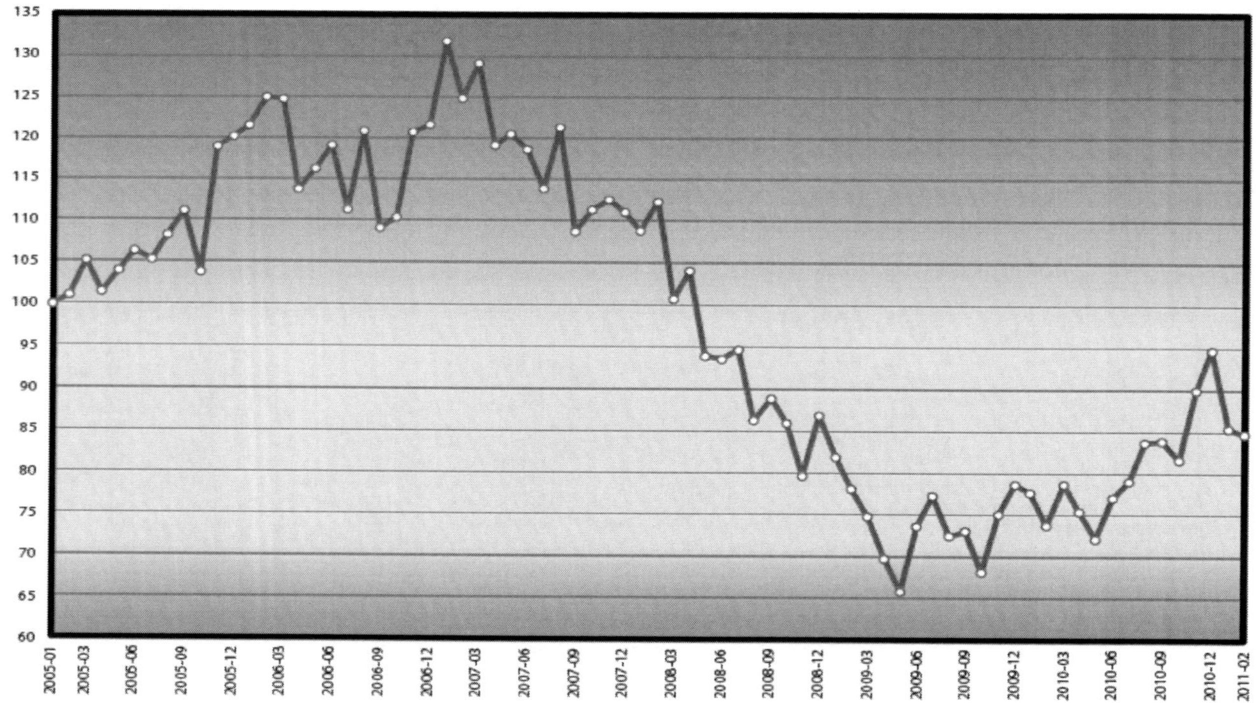

Source: PayNet/Thomson Reuters.

Figure 9. PayNet/Thomson Reuters Small Business Lending Index.

(Quarterly data, 1991-2011)

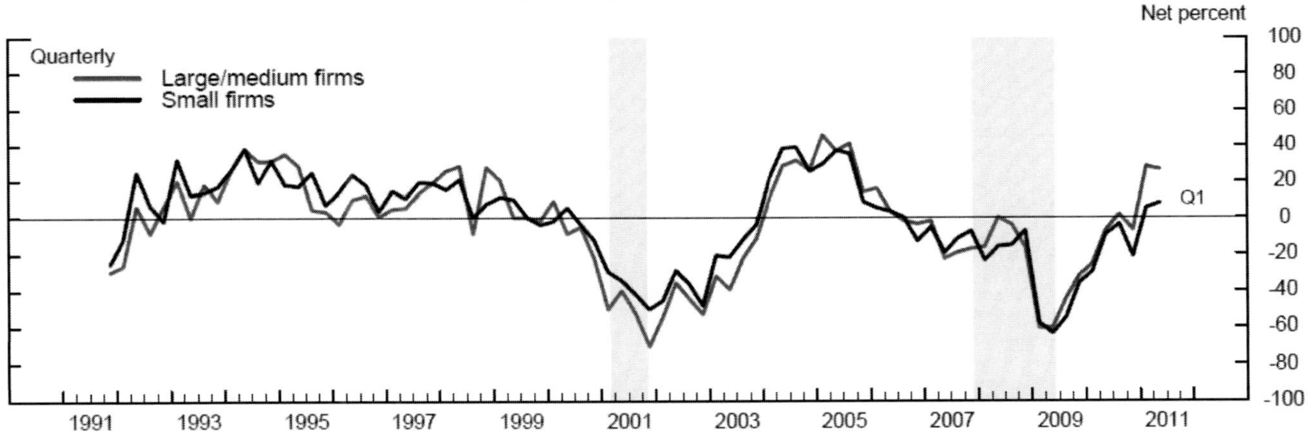

Note: Shaded areas denote National Bureau of Economic Research recession periods.
Source: Senior Loan Officer Opinion Survey on Bank Lending Practices, Federal Reserve Board.

Figure 10. Change in demand for consumer and industrial loans.

CONCLUSION

To sum up, the financial conditions that would be necessary for small businesses to start up and thrive would include positive conditions for personal wealth building and a full range of consumer and business credit availability. In the wake of the financial crisis, small business owners and potential small business owners likely experienced a substantial reduction in the personal resources necessary to start or sustain a business. At the same time, small business loans became harder to get, and when they were available, both price and nonprice credit terms were likely quite restrictive. Many small business owners were so convinced that their requests would be denied that they did not even apply for credit. Despite this restricted credit availability, small business owners, by a large margin, still considered their most significant problem to be weak sales. Although no definitive data source exists, the combination of a variety of recent survey results paints a picture of increasing optimism about future sales and business conditions and a corresponding easing of credit availability for small businesses.

End Notes

[1] See John C. Haltiwanger, Ron S. Jarmin, and Javier Miranda (2010), "Who Creates Jobs? Small vs. Large vs. Young," NBER Working Paper Series 16300 (Cambridge, Mass.: National Bureau of Economic Research, August).

[2] The report with the results of the 2010 SCF is expected to be released in early 2012 after all data from the survey have been assessed and analyzed.

[3] Unlike the 2010 Survey of Consumer Finances, which is a point-in-time cross-sectional survey, the 2009survey is based on follow-up interviews with participants in the 2007 SCF that update their information. For a research paper that provides an overview of the 2009 data, see Jesse Bricker, Brian Bucks, Arthur Kennickell, Traci Mach, and Kevin Moore (2011), "Surveying the Aftermath of the Storm: Changes in Family Finances for 2007 to 2009," Finance and Economics Discussion Series 2011-17 (Washington: Board of Governors of the Federal Reserve System, March).

[4] See Elizabeth A. Duke (2011), "Changed Circumstances: The Impact of the Financial Crisis on the Economic Condition of Workers Near Retirement and of Business Owners," speech delivered at the Virginia Association of Economists Sandridge Lecture, Richmond, Va., March 24,www.federalreserve.gov/newsevents/speech/duke20110324a.htm.

[5] The data are from the quarterly Call Reports, which ask banks to report their holdings of C&I loans made in original amounts of less than $1 million.

[6] See Alicia Robb and E.J. Reedy (2011), *An Overview of the Kauffman Firm Survey: Results from 2009 Business Activities* (Kansas City, Mo.: Ewing Marion Kauffman Foundation, March), www.kauffman.org/newsroom/lost-sales-and-tighter-lending-restrictions-challenge-young-firms-in-post-recession-economy-according-to-kauffman-study.aspx.

[7] In this and later figures, shaded bars indicate periods of business recession as defined by the National Bureau of Economic Research.

[8] National Small Business Association (2011), *2010 Year-End Economic Report* (Washington: NSBA), www.nsba.biz/docs/2010_ye_economic_report.pdf.

[9] Thomson Reuters provides some statistical tests showing that changes in the prior month's Small Business Lending Index values can predict the current month's change in the U.S. Leading Economic Indicators Index. See Andrew Clark and Thomas Ware (2010), "Looking into the Future with the Thomson Reuters/PayNet Small Business Lending Index (SBLI)," white paper (Thomson Reuters, May).

INDEX

A

B

C

D

E

F

G

H

I

T

U

V

W

Y